ANDRÉS BARBA was born in Madrid in 1975. He first gained renown in 2001 with *La hermana de Katia*, which was shortlisted for the Premio de Herralde and brought to the big screen by Mijke de Jong. His reputation as one of the most important Spanish writers of his generation was confirmed by the novels that followed: *Ahora tocad música de baile*; *Versiones de Teresa* (winner of the Premio Torrente Ballester); *Such Small Hands*; *August, October*; *Death of a Horse* (winner of the Premio Juan March); *En presencia de un payaso*; and *A Luminous Republic* (winner of the Premio Herralde and shortlisted for the Premio Gregor von Rezzori). He has also written essays and poetry and has translated into Spanish the works of authors including Herman Melville, Henry James, Joseph Conrad and Thomas De Quincey. He was chosen by *Granta* magazine as one of the best young Spanish-language novelists and his work has been translated into twenty-four languages.

LISA DILLMAN is professor of pedagogy at Emory University. In 2016 she won the Best Translated Book Award for Yuri Herrera's *Signs Preceding the End of the World*. In 2017, her translation of Andrés Barba's *Such Small Hands* was awarded the Oxford-Weidenfeld Translation Prize.

ALSO BY ANDRÉS BARBA FROM GRANTA BOOKS

Such Small Hands

A

LUMINOUS

REPUBLIC

ANDRÉS BARBA

Translated from the Spanish
by Lisa Dillman

With a foreword by
Edmund White

GRANTA

Granta Publications, 12 Addison Avenue, London W11 4QR

First published in Great Britain by Granta Books, 2020
This paperback edition published by Granta Books, 2021
First published in the United States in 2020 by Mariner Books,
Houghton Mifflin Harcourt, New York.

Copyright © 2017 by Andrés Barba
English translation copyright © 2020 by Lisa Dillman
Foreword copyright © 2020 by Edmund White

Originally published in Spanish by Editorial Anagrama as
República luminosa, 2017

Andrés Barba and Lisa Dillman have asserted their moral rights under the
Copyright, Designs and Patents Act, 1988, to be identified as the author and
translator respectively of this work.

All rights reserved. This book is copyright material and must not be copied,
reproduced, transferred, distributed, leased, licensed or publicly performed or
used in any way except as specifically permitted in writing by the publisher, as
allowed under the terms and conditions under which it was purchased or as
strictly permitted by applicable copyright law. Any unauthorized distribution
or use of this text may be a direct infringement of the author's and publisher's
rights, and those responsible may be liable in law accordingly.

A CIP catalogue record for this book is available from the British Library.

1 3 5 7 9 10 8 6 4 2

ISBN 978 1 84627 694 1
eISBN 978 1 84627 696 5

Book design by Margaret Rosewitz
Offset by Avon DataSet Ltd, 4 Arden Court, Alcester, Warwickshire B49 6HN
Printed and bound by CPI Group (UK) Ltd, Croydon, CR0 4YY
www.granta.com

For Carmen,

who is made of red earth

WALTHAM FOREST LIBRARIES	
904 000 00700792	
Askews & Holts	09-Jul-2021
AF	ⁿ

I am two things which cannot be ridiculous: a child
and a savage.

— PAUL GAUGUIN

FOREWORD

Edmund White

Andrés Barba's *A Luminous Republic* is one of the best books I've ever read (and I've read *lots* of books, thousands and thousands in my eighty years). Straight men in the seventies would always begin an article "I, a heterosexual," if they reviewed and liked one of my books. Let me just as comically say, "Barba, a platonic friend, a heterosexual married man," since my name, if known at all, can be a curse in some circles. We live in such a barbarous age of identity politics one can't be too explicit.

I suppose a Hollywood hack pitching this novel would say: *Lord of the Flies* meets *Heart of Darkness*. That would give only the crudest suggestion of this miraculous book, which is at once so strong and delicate that music alone comes to mind as a correlative—in Marianne Moore's line, "Like Gieseking playing Scarlatti," or more like Michelangeli playing Debussy—powerful chords hammered out amidst the most feathery ornaments.

What on earth am I talking about?

This is a story that takes place in the late twentieth and early twenty-first centuries, narrated by a youngish widower who arrived twenty years earlier, on April 13, 1993, as a civil servant with his wife and her daughter in San Cristóbal, a small mythical city in South America bordering the jungle. There is an air of magic, black and white, lingering around every page of this epic novel of 192 pages, like gun smoke after a shootout. I say "epic" because it feels as full, as dense with duration, as if it were 1,000 pages long but can be read in an evening.

It is about a provincial city where "wild" children, speaking their own language and seemingly without a leader, children between the ages of seven and thirteen, appear to be given over to joy and freedom. Where do they live? No one knows. Are they peaceful? It seems so, until they stab to death two adults in a raid on a supermarket "because of some glut of euphoria and ineptitude." They aren't just hungry; they are anarchic. When the city gives baskets of food to the city's poorest citizens on Christmas Eve, the children rip them open and scatter the treats.

This is the world that most rebellious children fantasize about. They're elusive, triumphant, opposed to the dull order that hangs over the city, erotic if not yet sexual.

Early on, we the readers are warned that all thirty-two of these jungle boys and girls will die, though we don't yet know why or how.

If portraits are paintings where something is wrong with the mouth, novels are usually books where something is wrong with the end.

Not this one! The ending is one of the most transcendent and beautiful I know of, a perfect dénouement but also as visually resplendent as Gozzoli's *Procession of the Magi* in Florence.

Most writers lose touch with childhood. Since I read Spanish badly, I can't claim to be a Barba completist, but the books I've read in English deal with children as wise as they are cruel, even perverse. Andrés Barba was born in 1975. He studied philosophy in university and can write thoughtful observations: "The world of childhood was crushing us with its preconceived notions, which is why a large part of the irritation people felt for the thirty-two had less to do with whether it was natural for children to have perpetrated an act of violence than it did with the rage triggered by the fact those very children had not confirmed their sugar-coated stereotypes of childhood."

Barba has written many books, including poetry, and translated more, including *Moby-Dick* and *Alice in Wonderland*. He won the Premio Herralde for this novel, which will be translated into twenty languages. *A Luminous Republic* shows a childhood of freedom and anarchy. (How Nietzsche would have loved this novel!) This is a book at once heavy and light, Caliban and Ariel, somber and comic. It will open your eyes.

EDMUND WHITE has written thirty books, including the forthcoming *A Saint from Texas*.

A

LUMINOUS

REPUBLIC

When I'm asked about the thirty-two children who lost their lives in San Cristóbal, my response varies depending on the age of my interlocutor. If we're the same age, I say that understanding is simply a matter of piecing together that which was previously seen as disjointed; if they're younger, I ask if they believe in bad omens. Almost always they'll say no, as if doing so would mean they had little regard for freedom. I ask no more questions and then tell them my version of events, because this is all I have and because it would be pointless to try to convince them that believing, or not, is less about their regard for freedom than their naïve faith in justice. If I were a little more forthright or a little less of a coward, I'd always begin my story the same way: *Almost everyone gets what they deserve, and bad omens do exist.* Oh, they most certainly do.

The day I arrived in San Cristóbal, twenty years ago now, I was a young civil servant with the Department of Social Affairs in Estepí who'd just been promoted. In the space of a few years I'd gone from being a skinny kid with a law degree to a recently married man whose happiness gave him a slightly more attractive air than he no doubt would otherwise have had. Life struck me as a simple series of adversities, relatively easy to overcome, which led to a death that was perhaps not simple but was inevitable and thus didn't merit thinking about. I didn't realize, back then, that in fact that was what happiness was, what youth was and what death was. And although I wasn't in essence mistaken about anything, I was making mistakes about everything. I'd fallen in love with a violin teacher from San Cristóbal who was three years my senior, mother of a nine-year-old girl. They were both named Maia and both had intense eyes, tiny noses and brown lips that I thought were the pinnacle of beauty. At times I felt they'd chosen me during some secret meeting, and I was so happy to have fallen for the pair of them that when I was offered the opportunity to transfer to San Cristóbal, I ran to Maia's house to tell her and asked her to marry me then and there.

I was offered the post because, two years earlier in Estepí, I had developed a social integration program for indigenous communities. The idea was simple and the program proved to be an effective model; it consisted of granting the indigenous exclusive rights to farm certain specific products. For that city we chose oranges and then tasked the indigenous community with supplying almost five thousand people. The program nearly descended into chaos when it came to distribution, but in the end the community rallied and after a period of readjustment created a small and very solvent cooperative which to this day is, to a large degree, self-financing.

The program was so successful that the state government contacted me through the Commission of Indigenous Settlements, requesting that I reproduce it with San Cristóbal's three thousand Ñeê inhabitants. They offered me housing and a managerial post in the Department of Social Affairs. In no time, Maia had started giving classes at the small music school in her hometown once more. She wouldn't admit it, but I knew that she was eager to return as a prosperous woman to the city she'd been forced by necessity to leave. The post even covered the girl's schooling (I always referred to her as "the girl," and when speaking to her directly, simply "girl") and offered a salary that would allow us to be-

gin saving. What more could I have asked for? I struggled
to contain my joy and asked Maia to tell me about the jungle, the river Eré, the streets of San Cristóbal . . . When she
spoke, I felt as if I were heading deeper and deeper into
thick, suffocating vegetation before abruptly coming upon a
heavenly Eden. My imagination may not have been particularly creative, but no one can say I wasn't optimistic.

We arrived in San Cristóbal on April 13, 1993. The heat
was muggy and intense and the sky completely clear. As we
drove into town in our old station wagon, I saw in the distance for the first time the vast brown expanse of water that
was the river Eré and San Cristóbal's jungle, an impenetra-
ble green monster. I was unaccustomed to the subtropical
climate and my body had been covered in sweat from the
moment we got off the highway and took the red sand road
leading to the city. The drive from Estepí (nearly a thousand kilometers) had sunk my spirits into a deep state of
melancholy. Arrival had, at first, been dreamlike, but then
abruptly taken on the ever harsh contours of poverty. I'd
been expecting the province to be poor, but true poverty re-
sembles the imagined sort very little. At the time I didn't yet
know that in the jungle poverty is leveled, that the jungle
normalizes and, in a sense, erases it. One of the city's mayors
said that the problem with San Cristóbal is that the sordid is
always but a small step from the picturesque. This is quite
literally true. Ñeê children's features are very photogenic

despite—or perhaps because of—the grime, and the subtropical climate encourages the magical thinking that their condition is somehow inevitable. To put it another way: a man can fight another man, but not a torrent or an electrical storm.

But I'd also noticed something else from the station wagon window: that San Cristóbal's poverty could be stripped to the bone. The colors were flat, vital and insanely bright: the jungle's intense green, which ran up to the road like a wall of vegetation, the earth's brilliant red, the blue sky so dazzling it forced you into a constant squint, the dense brown of the river Eré extending four kilometers shore to shore—all of it signaling so clearly that I had nothing in my mental repertoire with which to compare all that I was then seeing for the first time.

When we reached San Cristóbal we went to city hall for the keys to our house, and a civil servant came along in the station wagon to show us the way. We were nearly there when suddenly I saw, less than two meters away, a huge German shepherd mix. The feeling I got—no doubt induced by exhaustion from the trip—was almost phantasmagorical; it was as though, rather than having crossed the street, the dog had simply materialized in the middle of it, out of nowhere. There was no time to brake. I gripped the wheel as tightly as I could, felt the impact in my hands and heard a sound that no one who has heard it could ever forget—that of a body slamming into the bumper. We jumped out of the car. It was a female dog, badly injured, panting and avoiding our eyes as if ashamed of something.

Maia bent over her and stroked her back, and the dog responded with a slight wag of her tail. We decided to take her straight to a veterinarian, and on the way, in the same station wagon that had hit her, I got the feeling that this wild stray was two contradictory things at once: a benign presence and a terrible omen, a friend welcoming me to the city but also a messenger delivering alarming news. It struck me that even Maia's face had changed since our arrival, and was now both more common—never had I seen so many women who looked like her—and more concentrated; her skin looked softer and at the same time tougher, her expression both harder and less rigid. Maia had put the dog on her lap and blood had begun to soak her pants. The girl was in the back seat, eyes glued to the wound. Every time the car drove over a pothole the dog turned and let out a musical whimper.

They say either you have San Cristóbal in your blood or you don't, a cliché used for hometowns all over the world, but here it has a less mundane and more extraordinary dimension. Because, of course, blood is exactly what has to acclimatize to San Cristóbal, what must change temperature and succumb to the force of the jungle, of the river. The Eré itself, all four kilometers wide, has often struck me as a vast river of blood, and there are trees in this part of the country whose sap is so dark it's almost impossible to think of them as plants. Blood courses through everything, it *fills* everything. Beneath the green jungle, beneath the brown river, beneath the red earth there is always blood, a blood that flows and completes things.

My baptism, therefore, was literal. When we got to the veterinarian, the dog had almost no chance and, as I carried her in my arms, I became soaked with a viscous liquid that turned black upon contact with my clothes and gave off a repulsive saline odor. Maia insisted on getting the wound on the dog's hindquarters stitched up and having her leg put in a cast, and the animal closed her eyes as if to say she had no intention of putting up any more fight. Her closed eyes seemed to flit nervously beneath their lids, like humans when they dream. I tried to imagine what she might be seeing, what kind of wild jungle adventure she might be reproducing in her brain, and wished for her recovery and survival as if my own safety here were largely dependent on it. I approached her and put a hand on her hot snout in the belief, maybe even the conviction, that she would understand me and stay with us.

Two hours later the dog was on the patio of our house, eyes watering, and the girl was making her a plate of rice and leftovers. We sat together and I told her to come up with a name. The girl scrunched up her nose—her natural expression when dramatizing indecision—and said, "Moira." And that's still her name as she dozes a few feet from me all these years later, an old dog lying in the corridor. Moira. Considering that, against all predictions, she has outlived half the family, perhaps it's not so unlikely that she'll outlive us all. Only now do I understand her message.

Each time I try to recall how those first few years in San Cristóbal played out, what comes to mind is a piece Maia always struggled with on the violin: "The Last Rose of Summer," by Heinrich Wilhelm Ernst, a sort of traditional Irish ditty that had also been set to music by Beethoven and Britten and in which, it would seem, two separate realities can be heard: one, a somewhat sentimental melody, and the other a staggering display of technique. The contrast between San Cristóbal and the jungle was akin to those two realities: the first, the utterly relentless, utterly inhuman reality of the jungle, and the other a simple truth, one that was perhaps less true but certainly more practical, one we managed to live with.

It must be said that San Cristóbal was no great surprise: a provincial city of two hundred thousand, with its traditional families (known here as "old" families, as though some families were actually more aged than others), its political imbroglios and its subtropical torpor. I adapted to it better and more quickly that I had imagined. Within a few months, I was fighting like a local: battling staff absenteeism, the impunity of certain politicians and the type of provincial dilemmas that more often than not are inherited, convoluted and unsolvable. Maia, in addition to offering classes at the music school, was also teaching a few of San Cristóbal's well-to-do young señoritas, arrogant and nearly always very attractive girls. She'd rekindled her friendship with two or three women who fell silent as tombs if ever I walked in but whose voices I could always hear, talking over one another, as I approached. Like Maia, they were classical music teachers of Ñeê origin, and together they had formed a string trio. They held recitals — in the city and nearby towns — whose resounding success had less to do with their being good performers, perhaps, than it did with the fact that they were the only ones giving them.

What had for years struck me as an amusing contradiction in my wife's character—that she should devote herself to classical music yet only consider "real" the kind she could dance to—became perfectly comprehensible to me then. Classical music did not possess (either for her or for anyone else attending their concerts) the quality of music so much as that of stagnation. It was composed according to criteria too distant and by minds too different for this to be any other way, but that didn't make the audience unsusceptible to its influence. When Maia played those pieces, they wore the same concentrated expressions they'd have worn while listening to a foreign language, one that was particularly seductive and yet nonetheless incomprehensible. Ultimately, the reason Maia devoted herself so passionately to playing and teaching classical music was because she saw it as foreign, and she was incapable of any sentimental attachment to it. For Maia, classical music was something that took place only in the brain, while other types of music— cumbia, salsa, merengue—did so in the body, in the stomach.

One sometimes thinks that for a voyage to the depths of the human soul one needs a powerful submarine, and in the end is surprised to find oneself in a wetsuit trying to sink into a standard household bathtub. The same is true of places. If there's one thing that characterizes small cities, it's that they're as alike as tacks: it makes no difference which; they all use the same mechanisms to perpetuate power, the same circuits of legitimization and cronyism, the same dynamics. What's also true is that every once in a while, they each produce their own little local heroes: an exceptional musician, a judge from a particularly revolutionary family or a Mother Courage, but even those little heroes seem built-in, part of a system that in fact requires their very rebellion in order to keep perpetuating itself. Life in small cities is as synchronized and predictable as a metronome, and at times it's as difficult to imagine averting this fate as it is to believe that the sun rises in the west. But sometimes that's exactly what happens: the sun rises in the west.

Everyone sees the attack on Dakota Supermarket as the beginning of the trouble, but the problem began much earlier. *Where did the children come from?* The best-known documentary on the subject, the biased if not outright spurious *The Kids* by Valeria Danas, opens with a pompous voice-over asking that very question while showing bloody images from the supermarket: *Where did the children come from?* And yet it's true; this does continue to be the big question. Where? Anyone who'd never known a time when they weren't around could almost have thought that the children had been running through our streets forever, grimy and yet strangely, diminutively dignified, with their wild frizzy hair and sunburned faces.

It's hard to pinpoint the moment when our eyes started to become accustomed to them, or to know whether the first few times we saw them we were shocked. Of the many theories out there, perhaps the least absurd was the one proposed by Víctor Cobán, in one of his columns for *El Imparcial,* when he said that the kids "trickled in" to the city and at first blended in with the Ñeê children we were used to, the ones selling wild orchids and limes at traffic lights. Certain species of termite have the ability to change their appearance temporarily, taking on the characteristics of other species in order to penetrate a foreign environment and then reverting to their true appearance once they've become established. Perhaps the children, with the same pre-verbal intelligence as insects, adopted this strategy too, doing everything possible to resemble the Ñeê children we were already familiar with. But even if that were the case, the question would remain: Where did they come *from*? And, what's more, why were they all between nine and thirteen years old?

The simplest, but also the least proven, line of reasoning is that they were from all over the province, kids who'd been kidnapped by a trafficking ring and held in the jungle someplace near the river Eré. It wouldn't have been the first time. A few years earlier, in 1989, seven teenage girls about to be "distributed" to brothels all over the country had been rescued, and the photos the police took when they found them at a small ranch in the middle of the jungle just three kilometers from San Cristóbal were still fresh in the collective memory. Just as certain events preclude any naïveté, those images created a clear before and after in San Cristóbal's consciousness. It wasn't just that people were forced to recognize an undeniable social reality, it was that the shame this reality produced had been subsumed into San Cristóbal's collective consciousness in the same way traumatic events leave their mark on families: silently.

That was why people assumed these children had escaped from a similar type of "barracks" and turned up in the city from one day to the next. The theory—I repeat, baseless—was grounded in the ignoble distinction of San Cristóbal as the top province for kidnapped children, but it also had the virtue of explaining the supposedly "incomprehensible" language spoken by the thirty-two, which at the time was taken to be a foreign language. Nobody back then seemed to realize one simple thing: that buying into this theory would have meant that child mendicancy had increased by 70 percent overnight without sounding any sort of alarm.

After reviewing minutes from the meetings held by the Department of Social Affairs (of which, as I've said, I was in charge over the course of those months), I see that the first time child mendicancy appears as an agenda item is October 15, 1994, which is twelve weeks prior to the attack on Dakota Supermarket. This means—considering how slowly real problems in San Cristóbal made their way onto institutional terrain — that the children's presence in the city must have been noted two or three months earlier at least, which is to say in July or August of that year.

The theory that they escaped en masse from some jungle camp is so flawed that the "magical theory" that people had previously so derided, the one put forth by Ñeê community representative Itaete Cadogán, is almost more credible. He claimed that the children had "sprung" from the river. And if we don't take "spring" literally, perhaps it's not entirely implausible to imagine that something suddenly occurred in their consciousness, something that united them and led them to congregate in the city of San Cristóbal. Today we know that although over half of the children came from towns and cities near San Cristóbal (and that only a very small percentage of them had been kidnapped), others had inexplicably traveled over a thousand kilometers from cities like Masaya, Siuna and San Miguel del Sur. When their bodies were identified it was learned that two were from the capital, children whose disappearances had been reported to authorities months earlier and whose lives revealed nothing particularly suspicious until the moment they "ran away."

Extraordinary situations require us to reason with a different logic. Someone once compared the children's appearance to the fascinating synchronized flight of a starling murmuration: flocks of up to six thousand birds can form a dense cloud in the blink of an eye, swooping and turning up to 180 degrees in unison. I remember one occasion which, for some reason, has remained intact in my mind all this time. It took place during one of the months in which they must have arrived. I was in the car with Maia quite early, driving to my office at city hall. Work schedules in San Cristóbal are very rigid owing to the heat: people get up at six and life literally begins at dawn; official working hours are from seven to one o'clock, when the heat tends to be unbearable. During the harshest hours — from one to four thirty in the rainy season — a subtropical torpor engulfs the city, but in the morning San Cristóbalites are as energetic as can be, though that's surely not saying much. Maia was with me that morning because she had to take care of some paperwork at the music school, and when we got to the traffic light on our way downtown we saw a group of ten- to twelve-year-olds, begging. They both were and were not like the usual kids. Unlike the regulars, simple and plaintive as they begged, these children had a distinct sort of haughtiness, almost aristocratic. Maia rummaged in the glove compartment for a few coins but didn't find any. One of the boys simply stared at me. The whites of his eyes glinted, cold and intense, and his dirty face was such a contrast to the glint that for a moment I was speechless. The light turned green and I realized that I'd had my foot on the accelerator the entire time, as though I couldn't drive off fast enough. Before doing so, I turned to him one last time. Out of nowhere, the boy gave me a wide smile.

What mystery causes our perception of an experience to be concentrated in some images and not others? It would be a comfort to admit that our memories are as arbitrary as our tastes, that they select what we remember as randomly as our palates decide that we like meat but not seafood, and yet something makes us sure that even this, or rather *this above all,* depends on some code that has to be deciphered and is in no way coincidental. The boy's smile unsettled me because it confirmed that there had been a connection between us, that something that had begun in me ended in him.

Over the years I've come to find that my traffic light encounter was in fact a very common experience among San Cristóbalites. When asked, they all end up recounting similar if not outright identical episodes: children turning their heads at precisely the moment the person looks at them or appearing when the person thinks of them, real or phantom apparitions that make their way into dreams and the next day are waiting at the same place they were dreamt of. Perhaps in the end it's not so unfathomable that when someone looks at, speaks to or even thinks of a person, that person inevitably turns toward the source of attention. Those kids —whose numbers at the time were still modest enough not to draw attention—began acting as a sort of energy vector; without knowing it, we were alert to them.

On numerous occasions the Department of Social Affairs as a whole, and I in particular, have been accused of not having foreseen quickly enough what was no doubt the start of a problem. This is not the most appropriate place to dive into the national pastime of "predicting" Monday's news in Wednesday's papers, but it goes without saying that within two months of the altercations the city was filled with experts on childhood mendicancy and apostles of common sense. The very people who wanted police on the streets after the attack on Dakota Supermarket suddenly became pictures of moderation, Zen masters who accused us, with a vehemence only criminals deserve, of not having "acted swiftly enough."

At another point in my life I might have defended myself. Today I admit there's an element of truth to the assertion, but even so, what would "swiftly enough" have meant to those people at that time? Locking the children up in the orphanage? Making a public appeal? Fomenting animosity against a group of kids whose greatest display of antisocial behavior at the time was to be hungry and homeless?

Some things occur more quickly and easily than one might imagine: altercations, accidents, infatuations. Habits, too. At the time, I was walking the girl to school every day, and on the way, we'd play a little game. It was so simple and had begun so organically that I came to believe we'd be playing it forever, that even after she'd grown up we'd still be playing it, me seeing the strange curve of her neck before me, then hearing her footsteps behind. Perhaps what was most fun about the game was the feeling that we weren't actually playing at all, that we were offering ourselves up to the other's gaze. It consisted simply of passing each other without saying anything, first me, then her, then me again, until we got to school. Whoever was in front would, for a few seconds, be a short distance ahead and then slow down to let the other pass. From time to time one of us would pretend to be a different person — a man in a rush, late to work, casting ostentatious glances at his watch; a girl whistling as she skipped; a police officer pretending to give chase — but most of the time we were simply us, walking a bit faster.

It's odd how important I came to find those moments, waiting for the girl to pass me with her little steps. It seemed my love for the girl — or my slight distrust and close attention, which so resemble love — was like the inverse of my relationship with Maia, which was also loving but contained no rituals or expectations. While what I loved about Maia was my inability to access her deepest thoughts, in the girl it was *this* that I most loved — this thing we repeated almost against our will, this space we had created together.

We were unlike other families at school in that I was not my daughter's biological father, and this became clear every day when we arrived: not only did we not physically resemble each other, we also said goodbye without much fuss, slightly embarrassed. At the time, I did not yet know something I now do: resemblance is far from the atomic framework of a nuclear family. To an adult and a girl who want to be real father and real daughter, a lack of resemblance is not—as people often think—a tragic fate; the world is full of incompatible families with identical features, and happy families stitched together like patchwork.

Before Maia came along, I saw children as small beings with whom I had to invent a relationship. I distrusted people who claimed a wholesale like or dislike of them, because even I—despite always having struggled in my dealings with children—had often had the experience of meeting one specific child who triggered my instant affection. I was partial to the daydreamers and the awkward and averse to show-offs, flirts and chatterboxes (I've always hated childlike qualities in adults, and "adult" ones in children), but the long-held preconceptions one has about children evaporate the moment an actual child begins to form part of one's life.

The girl shared with the children involved in the altercations one distinct quality: she didn't feel entitled to the things around her. This may seem a minor detail, but it's not. In general, children brought up in minimally stable environments feel themselves to be natural heirs to that which surrounds them: their parents' car is *their* car; the house,

their house, etc. Children don't run off with forks from their
parents' kitchen; that would be absurd, as the fork already
belongs to them. A girl doesn't steal her parents' clothes to
play with them while they're out. Possession, in a child's
mind, is pure fact, a category used to filter reality. The kids
in the altercation, however — the boys and girls we were
starting to see on the street every day, stationed at specific
traffic lights or sleeping in small groups by the shore of the
Eré, who then vanished from the city at nightfall — shared
with my daughter the knowledge that unlike so-called normal kids, they were rightful heirs to nothing. And because
they were not rightful heirs, they had to *steal*.

I italicize this word intentionally. Not long ago I over-
heard a female colleague at city hall say, "The thing about
the altercations is that in those years we only allowed ourselves to think *in hushed tones*." The word "steal," the word
"thief," the word "murder." We're surrounded by words
that until now we've spoken only in a whisper. To name is
to bestow a fate, to listen is to comply.

So, on October 15, 1994, as per item 4 in the minutes of the biweekly Department of Social Affairs meeting, Deputy Isabel Plante raised for the first time the issue of child mendicancy. Noted therein (and it's not difficult to recognize Madame Plante's tortuously populist syntax) are three reports of "assaults" on residents in different parts of the city: the first on the manager of a cantina in Villa Toedo, where several kids made off with the day's takings; the second on a middle-aged woman whose purse had been snatched right in Plaza 16 de Diciembre; and a third on the waiter at Café Solaire, who claimed to have been "harassed by a group of vandals approximately twelve years in age." The deputy began by stating the facts, immediately thereafter demanded that funding for the orphanage be doubled so as to provide the necessary protection for the children, and then blamed me directly for the social ills the city was facing. A veritable master class in populist dialectics: call attention to an already out-of-control situation, offer an unattainable solution and accuse the political adversary of being responsible for it all. But leaving rhetoric aside, Madame Plante's speech does shed light on the fact that the children's world had started to make us all uncomfortable.

In an essay about the altercations, titled "Vigilance," published on the first anniversary of the deaths of the thirty-two, Professor García Rivelles dedicates one long section to the myth of childhood innocence. "The myth of childhood innocence," she writes, "is a bastardized, facile, hopeful take on the myth of Paradise Lost. Saints, intercessors and vestals of an ersatz religion, children are charged with representing the state of original grace for adults." But these children, the ones who had silently begun overtaking the streets, bore little resemblance to the two versions of the state of "original grace" we'd known previously: our own children, and the Ñeê children. It's true that the Ñeê were dirty and unschooled; yes, they were poor, and San Cristóbalites, in their

shortsightedness, assumed that they were a lost cause, but
the fact that they were indigenous not only took the edge off
this state, in a way it also rendered it invisible. Regardless of
how pitiful, filthy and often virus-ridden they looked, we'd
become immune to their situation. We could buy an orchid
or a small bag of limes from them without becoming distressed: the Ñeê were poor and illiterate in the same way
the jungle was green, the earth red and the river Eré heaved
with mud.

Apart from this, there simply wasn't much to distinguish
us. San Cristóbal, in the mid-nineties, was a city not very
different from any other large provincial city. The lifeblood
of the region's economy, tea and citrus fruits, experienced
a considerable boom, small farmers and landowners began
farming for themselves, and this led to real upward mobil-
ity for the working middle class. In the space of five years
the city was transformed: small businesses prospered, and
with them, the people's savings and general frivolity. The
construction company that had built the hydroelectric dam
bankrolled a makeover for the riverwalk, and this entirely
changed the face of the city: the historic center ceased to be
the only place for leisure, and San Cristóbal began to live,
for the first time, "with eyes riverward," as the mayor of the
time took to saying so affectedly. In the new San Cristóbal,
it became common to see young mothers taking their children for walks, couples out strolling, and sports cars that

still didn't quite fit with the landscape, scraping their un-
dercarriages on the speed bumps that had been installed to
control traffic. Children—*our* children—were not only
additional props on this orchestrated stage, in a way they
were also the blind spot of people's arrogance. People were
so taken by their own sense of prosperity that the appearance of the children, the *other* ones, was patently irksome.
Comfort is something that sticks to one's mind like a damp
shirt, and only after making an unexpected move does it become clear that one is stuck.

And while rhetoric is one thing, there were also the facts.
Two days later I myself witnessed the first of numerous assaults. Maia and I had gone out for a walk and came upon
them while crossing the little park with the hill. There were
six in total, the oldest a girl of about twelve. Beside her, on a
bench, sat two remarkably similar-looking boys, twins perhaps, probably ten or eleven years old; two other girls sat
on the ground and seemed to be making a game of killing
ants. They had the same grubbiness one sometimes sees in
destitute children in large cities. And the attitude. They appeared to be distracted, but in fact were on the alert. I remember the oldest wore a russet-colored dress with some
design—trees or flowers—embroidered on the chest, and
that she looked at me for a moment and dismissed me.

Thirty or so yards away, we saw a woman of about fifty

crossing the park with shopping bags. For a second everything froze. I realized that in our minds, both Maia and I were trying to confront the sense that something inevitable was about to occur. The oldest girl stood. Despite her scruffiness, she possessed an almost feline limpidity and the kind of openness of body only seen prior to adolescence. She called the kids around her, and without a word they stood and approached the woman, walking quickly. The oldest girl stopped in front of her and said something. Her head barely reached the woman's chest, so the woman bent slightly, resting one of her bags on the ground; immediately one of the smaller kids took advantage of this, grabbing the bag and running off.

Complicity is not the way I'd characterize the situation. There was something too dark, too deep for that, a sort of tacit synchronization. The intuitiveness with which each of these children adopted their role in the choreographed robbery reflected something more than a practice run, a trial. One boy or girl would begin a sentence, another would finish it. When the woman realized they'd stolen one of her bags, she stopped speaking to the oldest girl and turned brusquely, a pause that the girl used to snatch the bag that was still in the woman's hand. The girl jerked hard, but the woman was unpredictably defiant. Not only did she not let the girl grab her bag, she yanked back so hard that the girl actually fell. Then one of the twins jumped the woman and grabbed her purse, as the other gave a little leap and swung savagely from her hair.

The poor woman cried out. A cry of pain, to be sure, but more of shock. The hair-yanking was so violent that it brought her to the ground, and the children took advantage of her fall to snatch everything and run off with their booty: the purse and two more grocery bags. When we reached the woman, her face still looked more disconcerted than humiliated. She stared at us, eyes wide as plates. "Did you see that? Did you?"

From then on we all saw the children regularly — on the street, in the parks, by the river, even in the historic quarter. In general, they roamed in groups of three, four or five — never alone and never in large numbers. The groups were rarely set, though two or three were recognizable: the girl's group was easy to identify because the other two boys, the ones who so resembled each other, were often with her. Another was comprised of four boys and two girls on the brink of puberty who wore skirts down to their ankles. A third group was made up exclusively of boys who were always accompanied by a dog, a white stray. In the videos that remain from those months, some of the groups are relatively easy to spot, in particular the one with the dog. And in certain pictures from the renowned *Wasted Childhood* exhibit by photographer Gerardo Cenzana (this being part of the cultural production that helped define the "official version" of the facts), one might get the sense that some of the children are actually "repeated," faces we were all familiar with, but even this much is hard to claim with any conviction. It may be that the feeling that these particular children were more recognizable was nothing more than a strategy employed by our troubled minds, attempting to establish patterns where in fact none existed.

But days went by and no one did much about it. I had already begun working on the Ñeê community program and was so busy that I hardly gave the issue any thought. In a sense, the thirty-two now formed part of our daily reality, and only from time to time and in unexpected situations were we struck by the realization that something had changed. For instance: I recall that at the time — I suppose because the book had turned up at home — I was reading the girl *The Little Prince* at night. As a child I had read it with some interest, but on rereading the book to my daughter I started to feel disgusted, which I found difficult to understand. At first I thought it was the affectedness that bothered me, the whole solitary existence of this boy and his world — the planet, the little scarf rippling in the wind, the fox, the rose — until I realized that this was a downright evil book, a wolf in three layers of sheepskin. The little prince lands on a planet where he meets a fox who says that he can't play because he hasn't yet been "tamed." "What does that mean—tame?" asks the little prince, and after a couple of dodges the fox replies, "It means to establish ties." "To establish ties?" the little prince asks, even more per- plexed, and the fox responds with this extraordinary gem of bad faith: "To me, you are still nothing more than a little boy who is just like a hundred thousand other little boys. And I have no need of you. And you, on your part, have no need of me. To you, I am nothing more than a fox like a hundred thousand other foxes. But if you tame me, then we shall need each other." A few pages further on, standing be- fore a field of roses, the little prince proves he's learned the cynic's lesson: "You are not at all like my rose," he says. "As yet you are nothing. No one has tamed you, and you have tamed no one. You are like my fox when I first knew him. He was only a fox like a hundred thousand other foxes. But I have made him my friend, and now he is unique in all the world."

It still makes me shudder, the way our ingenuousness at the start of the altercations so resembled the ingenuousness that led Saint-Exupéry to write those things. Just like the little prince, we too thought that our individualized love for our children transformed them, that even blindfolded we'd recognize their voices from thousands of other children's voices. And perhaps the inverse of that serves as confirma- tion: that the other children who slowly began occupying our streets were more or less indistinguishable versions of the same boy or girl, children who were "just like a hundred thousand other little boys" and girls. Who we didn't need. Who didn't need us. And who, of course, had to be tamed.

But reality persists, and not even that made them cease to be children. How could we forget, given that it was there that the whole outrage began? Children. And one fine day it turned out that they stole. "They seemed so innocent!" exclaimed some, but after that outcry came the personal affront. "They seemed so innocent and they deceived us, the little hypocrites." They were children, granted, but not like *our* children.

On the afternoon of November 3, 1994, Mayor Juan Manuel Sosa called an emergency meeting, in the boardroom, with Amadeo Roque, San Cristóbal's provincial chief of police; Patricia Galindo, the presiding juvenile court judge; and me. The mayor strode into the room and dropped onto the table a file folder that, judging by his expression of disappointment, made less noise than he'd hoped. Maia used to say that in San Cristóbal it takes only five minutes of power for a man to start looking like a cacique. Sosa may have been a good example of this phenomenon: he was neither smart enough to be dangerous nor harmless enough to be funny. He had what is often referred to as "the common man's common sense," and it was hard to know which was worse, his opportunism or the fact that he went about promising favors left and right.

Still, the events laid out by the chief of police were far from invented: a couple of officers had approached a group of kids who'd been hanging out in Plaza 16 de Diciembre for several days and had robbed several pedestrians. According to one of the officers, the children replied to their questions in "an incomprehensible language" and attacked them when they tried to take the younger of the two—who was about twelve, he claimed—to the police station. In the first account the officer maintained that one of the kids had snatched his gun and "fired wildly," but later the testimony of several witnesses forced him to admit that the struggle had in fact caused the officer himself to fire accidentally. The bullet had hit his partner, Officer Wilfredo Argaz, penetrating the man's groin, and he'd died several minutes later, opposite the medical facility.

The officer's name was Camilo Ortiz. He was twenty-nine, had been on the force for two years and was in jail awaiting trial for involuntary manslaughter. The deceased Wilfredo Argaz was thirty-eight, the father of two girls and had a record considerably more questionable than his partner's: two internal investigations for bribery and one charge of gross misconduct for abuse of authority while interrogating a detainee. He may not have been an angel exactly, but now, regardless, he was a dead angel. Camilo Ortiz was going to be brought to trial for having drawn his weapon without just cause, and although it seemed likely that he would avoid prison, no judge on earth could (nor did) exonerate him from a hefty indemnity and dismissal from the police force.

Thanks to the official statement we drew up at that meeting, the death of Wilfredo Argaz was passed off as a tragic and preventable accident occurring in the line of duty. Understandably, we strictly avoided any mention of the children and in the communiqué substituted "common criminals" in their place. By fateful coincidence, the famous singer Nina died that same afternoon, and her death garnered so much press that the demise of Wilfredo Argaz became little more than a footnote in the police report.

Argaz's wife, however, seemed disinclined to let things go so merrily. Two days after her husband's death she planted herself at the door of city hall showing obvious signs of intoxication and holding her daughters' hands, and stood at the mayor's window screaming "Murderers!" for nearly twenty minutes.

All my life, I have reacted poorly to public displays of sorrow. Every time I've been forced to confront them, I've gotten the uneasy sense that my brain was somehow obstructing all compassion, albeit against my will. I remember when my mother died, in the hospital, and my father threw himself on her lifeless body and began wailing. I knew he'd always truly loved her, and I had been so stunned by the pain that I could hardly speak a word, but still I couldn't help but feel the entire scene was oddly fake, and this upset me almost more than her actual death. Suddenly I stopped feeling, the room seemed to have gotten larger and emptier, and in the middle of that open space, it was like we'd all frozen, turned to stone. All I could think, over and over, was "Good performance, papá, very good performance."

Watching this woman shouting in the plaza, I had a similar feeling. Her disheveled hair, her two pre-adolescent daughters, her clear signs of inebriation — there was something so obscene about it that I wasn't even upset at my own lack of empathy. I looked down on her from the office window and it was as if the distance between us was cosmic. She screamed, and her screams made no sense. She alternated between insulting the mayor and Camilo Ortiz, who must have been able to hear the whole thing from his cell. I sat back down and continued working. The woman fell silent. There came an unexpected quiet, and then she started screaming again, but this time something quite different: "It was those kids! Those kids did this!"

It was quite strange. The indifference I'd felt until that moment vanished instantly, turning to hate. I felt as if this woman were standing in the plaza blurting out a secret I'd been keeping, something shameful that I had never dared to confess, something I'd been hiding for weeks. I jumped up, ran to Amadeo Roque's office and asked him how long he intended to let that whore keep screaming in front of city hall. The police chief stared at me in shock.

That whore.

It's funny, the way certain words possess a viciousness that can linger for years, biding its time, before seeking us out again, as intense as when we first spoke them. Even now, nearly twenty years later, those words are like monks who'd been waiting patiently inside their monastery to mortify me. The vengeance of memory.

Three days later, in his November 6 column in *El Imparcial,* Víctor Cobán proved himself one of the few people who saw what was going on: "Only someone as foolish as our mayor, Juan Manuel Sosa, could, at this stage, still doubt the catastrophe that will be upon us if a solution to the issue of the street children is not found. Perhaps the death of Wilfredo Argaz was nothing more than an isolated accident, but the entire episode serves as a metaphor. And metaphors are powerful: just as we don't understand the words spoken by these children, who disappear each night as if they'd never been in our world and who seem to have no clear leader, it seems obvious that their presence belies some purpose we have yet to decipher."

It was true: they seemed to have no clear leader. Maybe a few of the groups were occasionally "captained" by specific children, but their movements didn't appear to be orchestrated by any one single brain. Sometimes they met behind city hall and spent hours hurling themselves down a grassy embankment, laughing and getting up to do it again. When happy they were scarcely any different from our children. They gestured and clowned around to make one another laugh, or bounced up too quickly after rolling down the hill and fell on their behinds, to great revelry. I recall having smiled on many of those occasions myself, shocked that these were the same children we crossed the street to avoid whenever we saw them. Furthermore, it struck me that those children possessed a sort of joy and freedom that, in a way, our own "normal" children could never have attained, as if childhood were better expressed in their games than in our children's games, which were so full of rules and prohibitions.

Today it might seem a grave oversight, but in small cities like San Cristóbal, the police's priorities revolved around criminality, and at the time there was no actual proof that the children were criminals. The few times an officer happened upon them with their hands in the cookie jar and tried to nab them, they scattered instantly and took off in all directions. Later they would meet back up. It wasn't unusual, for instance, for two different groups to turn up at the same place accidentally, argue briefly and then one group would leave. Had they been obeying any sort of instructions, we should have seen two leaders coming to an agreement, but that's never what happened: they would deliberate in a totally disorganized and random fashion, as though for a moment they'd forgotten why they were there to begin with, and then separate once more, sometimes in slightly reconfigured groups. I remember once hearing their behavior compared to an organism's cells: they were individual, and yet their lives were completely subsumed by the republic, like bees in a honeycomb. But if in fact the children were truly a unified body, where was the brain? If they a hive, who the queen bee?

The other thing Víctor Cobán mentioned in his column —the way they disappeared at nightfall—was no less unsettling. It proves that we still didn't know that the thirty-two went into the jungle at nightfall. We now know that in those months they had settlements close to the Eré, less than a kilometer from the riverwalk, and that they shifted their encampment two or three times, all the way along that line, deeper into the jungle, but why they chose those places (aside from defending themselves from us, obviously) remains a mystery.

Would it all have been simpler if we understood what they said? Or rather, if they'd allowed us to understand them? Hard to say. There's an article by Dr. Pedro Barrientos, professor of philology at the Catholic University of San Cristóbal—impossible to read without smiling today—in which he claims that the children spoke a lesser version of Ñeê. Some also claimed, at the time, that they were using a new form of Esperanto, and there were still more idiotic assertions that, at the time, were made quite seriously, and with an air of authority.

One of the greatest tragedies about the altercations is that there is so little remaining acoustic evidence. You can hear their voices on some videos of the attack on Dakota Supermarket. They sound like trilling birds, the sounds they make almost indistinguishable, like the buzz you hear deep in the jungle, but if you close your eyes, you get the sense that the musicality of their phrases could easily be the conversation of everyday children: the cadence of exclamation follows that of complaint; resolute affirmations come after acclamations; complicated questions are followed by replies. And there's joy, as if those children had discovered the secret to joy that normal children struggled to find. Listening to them laugh, one gets the sense that the world has made good on something, simply by having been able to produce that sound. But we didn't understand a word.

In the months that the children roamed the streets, they

almost never addressed us, and when speaking among themselves they did so in hushed tones, whispering into one another's ears. If they asked us for "spare change," for instance, those easily recognizable words somehow morphed, sounding as if they were swollen from within. I'm no linguist, but I am astonished that such banal circumstances altered our subjective perception of language so radically. Sometimes I think the children could have been speaking perfect Spanish and still we wouldn't have understood them; we'd have continued to believe that they were speaking another language.

And yet every hieroglyph has its Rosetta stone. Ours had a first and last name. The San Cristóbal altercations would never have had any sort of objective dimension without a twelve-year-old girl named Teresa Otaño, from the Antártida neighborhood. Teresa, in a sense, was (and still is, although for very different reasons these days) a shining example of our city. Her mother was a housewife of Ñeê descent, her father a rural doctor from upcountry who, thanks to his reputation, had opened a popular practice in the center of town. She could easily have been one of the girls Maia gave violin lessons to: educated, perceptive and aloof despite her humble origins, Teresa Otaño was, at twelve, already given to a certain kind of classism that at the time, in our city, was in its infancy.

San Cristóbal's middle class, to provide a quick sketch,

was like that old fable about the three frogs—the optimist, the pessimist and the realist—who fall into a bucket of milk. "There's no way I could possibly drown in such a small place," thinks the optimist frog, but its apathy is ultimately what makes it the first to sink and die. "The optimist has died!" thinks the pessimist frog. "So how could I possibly be saved?" and that desperation leads to the pessimist's death. But the third one, the realist frog who has been kicking its little legs the whole time just to stay afloat, begins to flail more desperately at the death of its companions and suddenly feels something solid, firm enough to stand on and from there to jump. By beating its legs the frog has made butter, and thus its realism (or desperation) is what saves it. After decades of heroic effort and boundless tenacity, a good part of San Cristóbal's middle class had become well-to-do: families who'd had serious problems paying the rent on a shack ten years earlier could now afford to buy relatively well-situated land and build their own homes. Teresa Otaño, whether she knew it or not, belonged to that class. She and her little friends were in the habit of walking from Antártida—at the time nothing more than the promise of an affluent, jungle-adjacent community—to Sagrada Concepción School and eyeing with disdain the Ñeê children whose mothers dragged them by the hand to sell orchids.

Otaño published her childhood diary as a young woman, at the age of twenty-five, eleven years after the accident that killed the thirty-two. It became an instant bestseller, locally. A Machiavellian mind could not have more skillfully calculated its success: the altercations were still so fresh in our collective psyche that anything to do with the case guaranteed immediate sales. What's more, the diary had a unique angle: the perspective of a girl. A girl who'd been watching the children that had so ruffled us. Parallels were drawn immediately, and in a sentence more twisted than a contortionist's intestines, the foreword compared the book to *The Diary of Anne Frank*. I will grant that the Otaño girl had one talent: an uncommon measure of self-awareness accompanied the inevitable immaturity of her age. "Twenty years from now, when I read this, I'll think: When I was a girl, I was terrible," she writes on one of the first pages, reflecting on the idea of examining her diary with "total sincerity" —a phrase far beyond the cerebral capacity of the average twelve-year-old brain.

But Teresa Otaño did something even more extraordinary than prove herself an insightful rich girl: she cracked the linguistic code used by the thirty-two. The whole thing came about through a lovely series of coincidences. Often, some of the thirty-two, on their nightly journey back to the jungle, congregated next to Teresa's house, on one corner of Antártida Avenue. It was no more than a stop of sorts, a meeting place. At first Teresa, enthralled, simply makes notes, logging the days on which they appeared, whether there were three, four or five of them, what they were wearing, and so forth. She establishes patterns and identifies a few of the kids, and then one—whom she initially refers to as "Bangs" and by the end is calling "the Cat"—becomes the object of a pubescent crush.

The Cat, like many of the thirty-two—according to Teresa Otaño's diary—smoked constantly, with the kind of feverishness one sees in adult vices only when taken up by children. He must have been one of the older boys in the group, about thirteen. Teresa describes him multiple times, smoking as he leans against the wall by her front gate, looking *like a lost outsider.* At one point she describes a scene of budding sexual development that would delight any analyst: *He walked to the gate and I heard the sound of his zipper, his pee hitting the wall and the sound of him spitting. Then he leaned over and rested his head on the railing.* I think everyone knows full well that the success of Teresa Otaño's diary was due in large part to passages like this one, which are especially prevalent in the first part of the book.

Teresa, like many San Cristóbal children, was a precocious girl. She understood in some vague way that a yawning gulf lay between her way of enacting childhood and these other kids', that it wasn't simply a question of poverty or neglect but something deeper that she claims *hit her in the gut* (to use her words) and compromised her scale of values. Despite the naïveté of her words, she does articulate something that the society she lived in had yet to fully comprehend: *I think a lot, but I don't speak much.* Could there be a more accurate assessment of what was going on inside all of us? And then, elsewhere in the book: *When we see them on the street we pretend they're not there, but they watch us and say nothing, like vultures.*

The walks from her house to Sagrada Concepción School with her girlfriends became little adventures for young Teresa. *Today they ran right past us and I felt one of the girls brush my arm, felt the touch of her hair tickle me.* So near, so far. And a few weeks later she claims that one of her friends was told she couldn't walk to school alone anymore, that her parents were afraid—more evidence of the fact that even months before the attack on Dakota Supermarket, hostility toward the thirty-two was starting to have tangible effects throughout the city.

It's not always easy to ascertain which has more sway, something we find threatening or something we find alluring. At times the nature of these two is not so much opposed as it is nearly indistinguishable. In her diary, it becomes clear that Teresa is unable to resist temptation despite knowing that it might endanger her, and not only in a passive way: she saves half of her sandwich from lunch and then unwraps it later, as she passes the kids on her way home, pretending to be in her own world; she makes sure to be seen on the patio and play in the parts of her house that are visible from the street. So in the end, it's not so strange that she ends up falling for one of them. The Cat is simply that invisible spirit, distilled.

One of the most exciting parts of her diary comes in the entry from December 21, when she cracks their linguistic code. But to recount this, a bit of background information is required:

A few days earlier, the street kids (as the thirty-two were sometimes called by this point) had been behind an incident that forever put an end to the city's friendly or indifferent attitude toward them—if, in fact, such a thing had once existed. The Department of Social Affairs had decided, given the approaching Christmas holidays, that this year we would launch a solidarity campaign, and it was to have an "angelic" touch: the plan was for the basic necessities often distributed to help meet families' needs over the holidays to appear anonymously on the doorsteps of the most underserved households. This lunatic plan was of the sort sometimes hatched halfway through a meeting out of sheer boredom. Perhaps it would have been enough for someone to kindly remind us that we did not in fact live in Copenhagen. But since nobody did, and since common sense is only lost when most needed, on the night of December 20 —veiled in a secrecy that we were at the time proud of— more than three tons of foodstuffs were distributed (products bought with charitable donations and what remained of our annual budget) and left on the doorsteps of private homes, food pantries, shelters, and so on.

Dawn the next day was horrific. When the city awoke at approximately six o'clock, nearly all of the gifts that had been so carefully deposited the night before were destroyed. The thirty-two had ripped open packets of rice and flour and scattered them everywhere, tins of oil and bottles of milk were broken, cans were open and crawling with insects. When I left home on my way to city hall and saw what had happened, the aftermath nearly reduced me to rage. By my door lay packets of candy and caramels that had been thrown willy-nilly. Tooth marks were visible on some of them — not those of wild animals but the familiar, recognizable imprints of children's teeth, as well as tiny fingerprints. They'd drawn smiley faces in the flour and thrown rice all over the place. They hadn't bothered to hide their crime. This had been done out of sheer joy; they were playing. The scene was a veritable celebration of scandal. Had they at least eaten the food, or stolen it to save for later, the charitable intent that prompted us to distribute these products might have served some purpose at least. But the gratuitousness of the destruction was too much.

On the night of this watershed, a twelve-year-old girl listens from her bedroom as they discuss what happened while waiting for their companions so they can all return to their nocturnal hideout. There are, according to Teresa

Otaño, six of them: two girls and four boys, the Cat among them. Perhaps due to their excitement, they speak a bit louder than usual and Teresa can hear them clearly. At first it's nothing more than intuition, like a brain sensing that it's about to solve a math problem, and then the feeling fades: *I understand but I don't understand,* Teresa Otaño writes. And then: *Are they speaking langidiguage?*

Like hundreds of thousands of kids all over the world, Teresa Otaño had invented a secret language to communicate with her friends without being understood by others. It was quite rudimentary and based on the repetition of "idig," either between a word's syllables or at the start or end of any monosyllabic word she wanted to conceal. The word "language," thus, would be translated as "langidiguage," for instance; the word "pen" could equally be rendered as "penidig" or "idigpen." With this simple trick she and her friends had passed notes in class believing them to be encoded. The thirty-two had developed a similar system, albeit extraordinarily more sophisticated. Teresa Otaño finally manages to "understand" a few words and even simple sentences and realizes that they're talking about what happened that morning, when they destroyed our "angelic" deed. One of the older boys scolds the younger ones for not having saved something — food, no doubt — and the littler ones take turns blaming one another, until in the end one of them begins to cry. The Cat tells the crying boy to shut up already, and the boy replies, *I won't shut up, you're not the boss, nobody is boss.* More weeping and wailing, and finally (as per Teresa Otaño's testimony) a fascinating question: *So you always want us to tell the truth?*

Each time I reread this first semi-unintelligible conversation, "translated" by Teresa Otaño, I feel a sort of thrill, as though suddenly the barking of dogs or the squeaking of dolphins had been rendered into human words. The very idea that with a little more resourcefulness and common sense we'd have been able to understand what those children were saying to one another now strikes me as a loss greater than that of El Dorado or the secret of the pyramids. It's obvious that Teresa Otaño was nowhere close to understanding the entirety of their conversations, and that she filled in the blanks with words and phrases of her own invention, but she'd made a breach.

Much later, using the hours of chance recordings that had been recovered over time, sociolinguistics professor Margarita Cadenas produced a fascinating study called "The New Language," largely, and unfairly, overlooked outside of academic circles. Cadenas's thesis is bold and, albeit in part more imaginative than scientific, also tenable. According to her, the "need" for a new language for the thirty-two arose not out of the presence of any other group —that is, the children didn't choose to speak this way just to avoid being understood by others, as the young Teresa

Otaño and her classmates did — but out of a perfectly ludic and creative urge. Professor Cadenas believes that these children, given their new world and new life, had need of a new language: new words to name that which had yet to be named. She comes out against Ferdinand de Saussure's theory of the arbitrariness of linguistic signs, which claims that the relationship between a word and the object it denotes is random — that there is no logical reason why a table should inevitably be called "table" rather than "tree" or "plaza," which are equally random. The language that the children were "beginning to invent through codified games, employing Spanish as their base," she claims, actually functioned in the opposite way, by trying to find a place where the link was not arbitrary but triggered, a magical language in which the names of things sprang spontaneously from their very nature.

When a bird leaving the nest takes its first tremulous steps and jumps from a potentially fatal height, it is not making a philosophical statement on the art of flight, it's simply flying: this behavior obeys countless years of genetic input; the combination of movements has been produced in its brain before the first flap of its wings. It's clear that the thirty-two didn't hold a linguistics conference before using the first words of their new language. Cadenas's thesis is particularly firm on this point: their language was based on the concept of play. For them, the need for language

stemmed less from the need to communicate than the need
to play. They used Spanish as a foundation and then performed on it a syncretic act. They eliminated verb tenses,
reducing everything to the present indicative. Temporal information was expressed at the end of the sentence using a
generic marker. An utterance like "I went to your house"
would, according to Professor Cadenas, be reformulated
thus: "I go to your house yesterday." And although from a
structural perspective their language was syncretic—that
is, tending toward simplification and assimilation—from a
lexical perspective it was the opposite, tending toward creativity, chaos and multiplication.

Cadenas claims that in order to create new words, the
thirty-two would sometimes include—as Teresa Otaño did
—the random repetition of certain syllables and sometimes
alter the order of syllables, turning "time" into "mite," and
"simple" into "plemis," but often would also invent and
adopt new words out of the blue, which led to there being
two or three words for the same thing, all in use simultaneously. Of the latter group—the "triggered" words—we
know a few, thanks to Teresa Otaño's diary and the tenacity of Professor Cadenas, including "bloda" for "darkness"
(and "night"), "trum" for "community" ("family," "group")
and others such as "har" ("plaza" or "meeting place"), "mol"
("sky") and "galo" ("fight," "confrontation"). There is no
doubt that this language was in its very early stages, and not

even the thirty-two knew where it was going. How a group of children who, at the time, had been together for only six months — insofar as we know — managed to learn the rules of a new language so quickly and efficiently is a mystery deserving of its own tome, but I can think of no one more ill suited to writing it than me.

As for young Teresa Otaño, the girl spying at the window, it's almost impossible not to picture her there, still and alert. Her diary contains something far more notable than adolescent obsession with a group of *petits sauvages:* the inevitable scorn she feels toward anything she can't comprehend. Perhaps what's truly dark about all this is that she represented a collective sentiment, one that began there, in the feeling that no matter how often we saw them on our streets, how much we wondered about the meaning of what they were saying or where they hid at night, how afraid we were of them and how little we dared to admit it, those children had started changing the names of everything.

I once read that Hitler's real discovery after World War I was not, as is often thought, his ability to channel the fury and resentment of a nation, enlisting its citizens in his crazed project, but something far more trivial and almost banal: that people don't have private lives, men do not have lovers nor do they stay home to read books, in fact people are predisposed toward ceremonies, crowds and parades. Now that Maia is dead I've come to the conclusion that the true purpose of marriage is none other than talking, and this is

not only precisely what distinguishes it from other types
of personal relationships but also what is most missed: the
trivial conversations about everything from the neighbor's
bad mood to how ugly a friend's daughter is. Pointless and
none too insightful observations are the essence of intimacy,
what we mourn after the death our wives, our fathers, our
friends.

A few months after Maia's death I was tormented by the
idea that I didn't know my wife's secret pleasures. What
had been her small joys, her tiny compensations? The idea
that Maia's little secrets had died along with her produced
in me such anguish that I felt as if her entire existence had
been reduced to subatomic level. But there's always a thread
that can be tugged at, and quickly I thought of her hands
and the shapes they took as she explained to her pupils the
proper way to attack an instrument, according to either the
Russian or the French school, depending on what they were
attempting at a given moment: precision or emotion. Precision was in the arm, emotion in the hand, or better still, in
the fingers, the digits. And then I saw her fingers and also
recalled the concert at our house that Christmas of 1994,
and the girls.

Maia had established the custom long before she met me:
every year as Christmas drew near, she organized a concert for all her pupils. Each would prepare a piece suited

to their abilities, to be played for all the families. At the end she played too, with her string trio. I was always moved by my wife's face when she played, the sense that she was falling through space, but at a gentle speed, one that required enormous concentration. She would stand very erect on those fine round legs, one slightly in front of the other, and rest her head on the violin in such a way that I thought it looked like she was leaning on a cushion. Her cheek pressed to the instrument made her lips look slightly fuller, and because she always closed her eyes, or opened them just long enough to cast a quick glance at the score, it was as though her music were something that could be produced only from within relative darkness.

That day the recital was held on our patio, and in her habitual anti-Christmas spirit, Maia played Tartini's *Devil's Trill,* one of her favorite pieces, and one that she always performed well. Her students had played one by one in an unremarkable procession, and when it was Maia's turn I realized that the faces of three little kids, two boys and a girl, had appeared from within the hedges separating our house from the street. They must have been between ten and twelve years old and had pulled themselves all the way beneath the shrubs. Their hair was covered in weeds as they hid under the branches. They looked like three versions of the same wild animal, but their features were so fine and precise that to this day I recall them clearly. One of the boys had a very large, expressive mouth, the other droopy eyelids, and the girl — the oldest of the three — a squarish head with protruding ears and an exceedingly wary look.

The whole food donation fiasco had taken place shortly before, and at the time the press had taken their rage out on me. *El Imparcial*'s editorial cartoon had caricatured me as some sort of Pied Piper of Hamelin being followed by a swarm of ragged children. I was so upset that when I saw those three grimy faces peeking out from under the bushes, I took it as a personal affront and decided that I'd let Maia start playing and then catch at least one of them. How about a photo of me, firmly — not violently, but firmly — grabbing hold of the girl and escorting her to the San Cristóbal juvenile detention center? That wouldn't be a bad way to put an end to the whole matter before the holidays.

Maia began talking about the Tartini sonata. I'd heard her tell her pupils this story dozens of times. She explained that in 1713, as recounted to Jérôme Lalande, who later wrote of it in *Voyage of a Frenchman in Italy,* Tartini spent the night at an inn where he had a dream in which the devil appeared before him. After an unsettling conversation, he sold his soul in exchange for one wish: to become a famous composer. Anxious to put the devil to the test, he handed over his violin and requested that he compose something for him. The devil then played a baroque sonata so prodigious that Tartini had never heard anything like it in his life, and his awe caused him to wake in anguish. A moment later — not knowing whether he had in fact sold his soul to the devil for the piece or it had simply been a dream — Tartini transcribed what little he could recall of the melody by candlelight and titled it *Devil's Trill,* a fantastical piece.

Maia paused dramatically.

"A sonata composed by a man who was asleep," she added.

I saw how the children knit their brows in their hiding place. Their faces expressed an element of incredulity, but also gave the impression that something in their spirits had been won over: the devil, the dream, perhaps Maia's melodramatic storytelling, sprinkled with half-truths. The children's palms were pressed to the ground, their gazes fixed on Maia. I got out of my chair and approached, attempting to attract as little attention as possible. Maia started to play, and I leaned casually against a tree. From there I could see the girl's hand, poking out from the shrub like a mole's nose, and I decided that when Maia began the allegro I'd pounce and grab it firmly.

It all happened very quickly, and when I pounced my only thought was that I'd overstepped the mark. The first thing I noticed was that this girl's hand was extraordinarily small, and too hot. It was hard as stone yet had the familiar feel of a child's hand, and brought to mind the girl's hand, which I'd taken a thousand times when we went for strolls. I pulled hard and got her out easily. Rather than her face, what I saw was her mouth, open like a tiny well. She kicked and screamed so vehemently that for a second I thought it wasn't a human being I had in my arms but some sort of giant insect. I wasn't sure what I was holding her by: parts that seemed they should have been soft were actually hard, and her joints bent in unpredictable places. The girl shrieked unbearably, and when I tried to cover her mouth, her two friends leaped on me and began scratching my face.

Fear and thought have a strange relationship, as though the former were required to block the latter but also to instigate it. I didn't let go of her immediately, instead holding her hand forcefully in one of mine while covering my face with the other to shield myself. More than being scratched, it felt as if I were being struck with twigs. For a moment I lost my sense of direction and fell. At this point I let go of the girl and a second later it was over. Maia rushed to my side.

"Are you alright? Can you see me?" she asked.

"Of course. Why?" I asked, touching my eyelids, but as I brought my fingertips to my eyes, I saw that they were covered in blood.

The wound looked worse than it in fact was; once my face was washed, it turned out to be nothing but a few scratches. Still, the sense that those children had tried to poke my eyes out lingered into the night, first as a crazy idea and then as a dream. Like Tartini at his inn, I too was paid a visit: in my dream three girls like three little reapers approached and plucked my eyes out with their tiny hands. I didn't feel any physical pain, didn't react, the dream continued, and then suddenly I was blind and heard their voices. They sang and played all around me. The darkness, which had felt threatening, became pleasant. I felt inexplicably at peace, as though something inside them—or perhaps inside me—had finally abandoned the urge to solve a problem that had been troubling me. For some reason it was extraordinarily pleasurable to have freed myself of the need to see, and I curled up in my dream as if it were a warm, fluffy blanket. But then the girls approached and gently touched my head. A brief, childlike touch.

"You have to look," they said.

And then I opened my eyes.

Perhaps it was no coincidence that the attack on Dakota Supermarket took place after the holidays. The gulf separating the world of the happy from that of the sad is never so wide as it is during Christmas and New Year's. San Cristóbal has no snowy cabins, no stuffed turkeys, no Father Christmases. The heat is at its most suffocating in December, the rainy season one long mesa that goes from torrential rain to sweltering heat and back to torrential rain. Sheet metal roofs bake in the sun, turning homes into saunas. The heat and humidity mean that office work and bureaucracy take longer, people sleep poorly and less, and the yawning chasm between this place and actual civilization is made manifest. Only the Eré still flows impassively, like a fable whose moral hangs in suspense.

The attack on Dakota Supermarket happened precisely at this time of year, just one week after the holidays, on January 7, 1995. Press reports from January 8 are contradictory, but a rough picture can be sketched by piecing together all the news items published that day: a group of four children turns up at the supermarket entrance early in the morning, a relatively normal occurrence; they walk in, walk out, beg for food, leave the premises. At this point, January 7 is still, according to press reports, incident-free. But the children return at lunchtime. According to the Dakota manager's testimony, returning later was something they never did, and on that day, when they did so, it was not to beg: "They sat in the parking lot outside the supermarket and started playing." Some witnesses claim that these children were "a little older, twelve or thirteen"; others maintain they weren't playing but "arguing." All of the statements make baffled reference, at one point or another, to the same thing: the absence of a leader, a fact confirmed by all remaining video footage, images and documents of the children.

At one o'clock, they attempt to steal soft drinks and are caught red-handed by the security guard. It's shocking, even today, to watch the guard's brutal reaction and the passive — if not downright acquiescent — way the shoppers in the supermarket look on, captured by the security cameras. No one makes any attempt to stop the guard from slapping one of the boys repeatedly; no one stammers even the mildest reproach. This footage alone would have been enough for an international juvenile tribunal to send the man to prison after a summary trial, but there in the middle of Dakota Supermarket, in broad daylight and the presence of some fifteen "respectable" adults, on January 7, 1995, his actions produced no response whatsoever. The supermarket manager offers this unforgettable excuse to the press: "It might look like he went a little too far, but tempers were hot. Those kids came in here every single day."

An attorney would have responded to this with the "rule of minimum quantity," a basic law found in every penal system in the world and one which states that, given that crime is committed for the benefits it yields, in order for the punishment society metes out to produce the desired effect on the criminal, it must outweigh the benefits obtained by the commission of the crime. Put simply: a thief who steals two hens must repay three. It's a comprehensible law, but it launches sentencing into the realm of one's imagination, since it deems the efficacy of punishment to be grounded in its "unequal" condition. By forcing a thief to repay three hens for having stolen two, the law expresses faith not in redistributive justice or reintegrating the criminal into society, but in the disinclination other thieves will feel on seeing the punishment inflicted upon the first. Taking this to its logical extreme — and presuming there were some way to ensure that the criminal was incapable of reoffending — it wouldn't be necessary to punish thieves at all; it would be enough to keep them in isolation and simply make others *believe* they'd been punished. Imagining the thief's punishment would suffice. Over time, I've come to see that this is exactly what we should have done with the thirty-two: isolate one or two of them and then instill in the remainder the belief that we'd punished the missing children in some intolerable way. Perhaps picturing one of their number arrested and punished would have triggered indignation — or maybe a furious desire to rescue the missing — but in the long run it would have acted like a tumor in a young organism, the former feeding off the latter's energy.

But violence is not governed by predictable patterns. The January 7 camera footage is proof of that. The kids in the parking lot rebel, not right after the security guard episode but in a moment of calm. In the images we have (which include the victim assaulted by the guard), they go back outside and start playing as though nothing had happened. In the footage they can be seen out there for another thirty minutes. It's an odd game they play, like cops and robbers, but with some sort of captive. They split into two teams and then chase one child, who wears a T-shirt tied around his head. One team protects him while the other tries to catch him. Whenever they do, everyone dives, laughing and piling onto the boy or girl in the T-shirt.

The camera footage doesn't span the entire parking lot and at times they're out of the frame, but it's clear that more and more children start turning up. It's like a reverberation. What at first sounds strained becomes increasingly dialectical. The game comes to an end and they all lie down in the shade provided by a sign, an advertisement. There are twenty-three children present, the youngest no more than ten, the oldest probably about thirteen. They can be seen arguing in small groups, and it's also clear that the arguing grows heated. This is observable in their body language: suddenly nearly all of them are standing, hands on hips, on tiptoe and craning their necks to hear what others are saying. A few girls run from group to group, still playing. They slap one boy on the back of the neck and run off, laughing. There is no authority figure present, no one appears to be organizing anything, the groups are not enacting any sort of conspiratorial plot; they don't seem to be coming to any sort of agreement as far as strategy or elaborating a plan of attack. Quite the contrary: their anarchic movements are more suggestive of a game.

So why do more children keep arriving? How did they contact one another? At 2:40 p.m., twenty-eight children can be counted in the Dakota Supermarket parking lot. Barring the sinister image of thirty-two corpses taken by Gerardo Cenzana a year later in the sports pavilion, this may have been the most complete "group photo" we had up until that point. Girls comprise a third of the group, though it is not always easy to distinguish the sex of each child. They are all dressed quite similarly: T-shirts and jeans, or shorts. They are all dirty, although on balance less so than one might have imagined, which makes me suspect that the cliché about their lack of hygiene should also be reexamined.

When they enter the supermarket it is 3:02, as per the camera's time stamp. The security guard intercepts them at the door, pushes the first children a few times but is immediately stampeded by the miniature mob. The white dog that's always with one of the groups barks at an employee and bites the guard. Knives appear almost instantaneously, some snatched directly from the hardware section of the supermarket, others from behind the fish and meat counters. It's been said many times that the killers comprised only a small number of the community, that there were only five or six who took lives and the rest behaved like children throughout, a notion easily borne out by the security camera footage. The oscillation between chaos and regrouping, disorder and order, might be compared to the initial stampede and subsequent regathering of any group of children after being told that, if they wanted, they could destroy anything around them. The kids themselves seem disconcerted by the sudden freedom and look around at one another. Their first outburst is one of joy: in the dairy section, three boys concentrate on setting milk cartons on the floor and jumping on top of them so they explode; another boy empties a bag of flour onto a girl's head, and she begins to cry; one lone child rips into a packet of cereal, emptying it into his open mouth; two others knock wine bottles from the shelves with broomsticks. Had things ended there, it would have been impossible not to watch their shenanigans and smile; they're enacting a child's supreme dream: rising up and rebelling against adult organization. But at that precise moment, anyone's smile would freeze on their face. The butchery begins.

San Cristóbal police chief Amadeo Roque, the mayor, Presiding Juvenile Court Judge Patricia Galindo and I organized the camera images that very afternoon into three groups: group A were those images that under no circumstances should be in the public domain, given their criminal content; group B, those that could not be in the public domain because of the police investigation into events prior to the attack (namely, those from the parking lot); and group C, those that would be made public due to media pressure.

It's difficult to describe the nature of the first group of photos. On the one hand, they look like infantile chaos: the acts of violence (stabbings nearly all) are schematic, the victims fall as if, rather than actually having been stabbed, they were putting on a poor performance, or had been tripped. Many of the children remain grouped at the door, others even start crying and some bend over the victims while keeping a few feet of distance, as though drugged by the result of what they'd just done. The total duration of the attack is surprising, as are its clumsiness and the contrast between the various actions all happening simultaneously: during the almost ten minutes it lasted, some people leave and then come back in as if nothing were the matter, one woman takes advantage of the confusion to steal what looks to be a box of hair dye, while on the other side of the shelving a ten-year-old child has just sunk a knife into an adult's stomach. The theory — the most believable one, to me — that the children had no criminal intent before entering, and that the murders came about because of some glut of euphoria and ineptitude, is especially confirmed by these two elements: the duration and the disorganization. Had the attack been planned — even if it were *poorly* planned — it would have had a more efficient and less hesitant air about it, would have pursued a clear objective.

And the same way the violence sparks off, it seems to defuse. For four minutes, an impressive calm overcomes every person inside: the wounded drag themselves off, the kids regroup by the fish counter, some still with knives in their hands, others continuing to throw things on the floor, and one who stands frozen before a security camera, paralyzed, like a lonely pawn after a quick round of chess. What is the boy staring at so fixedly? It's impossible to know for sure what happened in this place, to breathe the actual oxygen of the space. Not even the tragedy's survivors could make sense of it, except with phrases ranging from the obvious to the incomprehensible: "It was a nightmare," "There's no explaining what happened . . ." Only after countless pages of platitudes come two statements that have the harsh and undeniable flavor of truth: one from a woman who swears that the kids had "insect faces" and another from one of the cashiers, who declares, "We all knew exactly what we had to do." Of the two statements, the second robbed me of sleep for months.

No less inexplicable is the outcome of the attack. The re- cordings show that when all of the children are congregated by the fish counter, something causes them to run pell-mell for the door. It's not an escape but a stampede. As though something, some insurmountable terror, had all of a sudden shaken them from inside.

At 3:17 it's all over. A crowd has gathered around the supermarket and the children have disappeared into the jungle. The tally: three wounded and two dead, a man and a woman, by stabbing. But there's something harder to count than the victims, something infinitely more palpable and definite, a feeling akin to terror: the conviction that this was but the first step of an irreversible process.

People pay the same sort of attention when they're afraid as they do when they're in love. This might seem a minor discovery, but making it in the days following the attack gave me the sense of bridging two continents poles apart. At home I often sat in the hall helping my daughter with her homework, and I'd stare out at the shrub where the three children's heads had emerged on the afternoon of the concert. I found it odd that, despite not really recalling their faces, the feeling they'd evoked was still so precise: it was as if I could sense their height, their contours, even their weight. Then I would look at my daughter's face and get the same feeling: as she bent over her notebook I'd watch the whites of her eyes and the lovely contrast they produced against her dark skin, her round forehead and the slant of her cheeks, her thick unruly hair.

"It's no wonder," wrote Víctor Cobán in a January 15, 1995, column in *El Imparcial,* "that we now look on our children differently, as though we've become enemies." And he was quite right. The desperate way we'd thrown ourselves into the search for those children and the anxiety we'd started to feel about our own had created common ground: the sentiment that began in the former inevitably ended in the latter, as though one were merely the inverse of the other.

In the course of those first few days there emerged three contradictory yet complementary reactions: shock, a desire for revenge, and pity. The passion for others' misfortunes was rekindled in the heat of the supermarket attack. The same pity masquerading as generosity and good intentions that many had shown for the children when they did no more than beg on the streets turned first to shock and then to malice. The victims' families camped out in front of city hall, demanding heads (mine among them), and forced us to hold an absurd plenary session in which we agreed to what could have been called a hunt, plain and simple, but given that it was for children, we decided to call it a search.

We were so sure we knew where their jungle encampment was that we didn't mind wasting a few hours to ensure that upon finding the children we'd be able to catch the greatest number possible. After all, we thought — as though we hadn't been mistaken on so many things thus far — they were only children and could not have gone far. Our aim was to make a single decisive entry, in a show of authority, and bring them back to be tried as juveniles. But the incident had such national impact that things got unexpectedly complicated. The camera images were so disturbing that they were circulated, shown on every television channel in the country. The city became a madhouse, overrun by journalists, and the locals' versions and the statements they made to police contradicted one another, people swearing they'd seen the children at their houses that same afternoon, and the following day, peeking into windows in the middle of the night, rummaging through their garbage after dark. The streets filled with reporters and cameras, and a mysterious urge to be in the limelight overtook several of the actual witnesses, leading them to make statements so outrageous that, had two people not been killed the day before, they'd have been frankly comical. Maybe they were. Many years after the altercations, Maia remarked that people in San Cristóbal had never stopped laughing, even when the most dramatic events took place, and at the time I was shocked to see how true it was and how unaware I'd been of the fact. Even on the most fraught days—and perhaps more so on those days—I could always think of a moment when I'd laughed. It wasn't simply a matter of our trying to lighten the mood by making nervous jokes; it was the seemingly improbable yet logical realization that it's impossible for us to watch nonstop coverage of a crime without something eliciting a smile sooner or later. Yes, we let off steam with a chuckle or two from time to time, but that doesn't mean we weren't in up to our necks. The useless machinery of internal bureaucracy had fallen upon us like a net covered in glue, the Ministry of the Interior was demanding justification for every decision made, and because the incompetence of Minister Balmes's cabinet was supreme, we couldn't get the item approved so as to undertake the search as quickly as possible.

At first light on January 11, a party of fifty police officers began to sweep the eastern shore of the river Eré. The children hadn't been seen around town again, leading us to assume that there was no place else they could be. Chief Amadeo Roque used a circular search pattern; this way, the moment anyone caught sight of the group, the police could tighten the cordon until they had the children ensnared. But the officers made it seven kilometers into dense jungle and found no other trace of them than two abandoned camps, a few articles of clothing, the remains of some food and a couple of toys. Fifteen hours into the operation, one of the officers was bitten by a coral snake and had to be carried out along the river. When the search party reemerged with no children and one officer with a tongue swollen up like a sponge, despair began to set in.

The jungle had swallowed up the San Cristóbal children, made them disappear. "If I was with them," a lovelorn Teresa Otaño writes in her diary on January 17, "me and the Cat would climb a tree and they'd never find us." Whether in the trees or the depths of the river, the children's whereabouts for those almost four months remains unknown. We can now establish some of their movements with a degree of certainty and trace a partial map of the areas where they hid, based on brief appearances they made at an inland tenant farm and two Ñeê settlements, but knowing this doesn't resolve much. We're similarly uninformed as to the nature of those encounters. Both the children and the communities in question are united in a common resentment of San Cristóbal, which makes it not unlikely that their contact was friendlier than they later claimed. But friendly or not, the encounters must have been few and far between, or we would have discovered them.

Human logic has a particular form of reasoning, and certain ideas don't seem to conform. "That can't be, it's too absurd," we might say. But that some ideas seem too absurd doesn't preclude them from being true. The San Cristóbal children's disappearance into the jungle was one of those, and the first thing this absurd conception did was leave us to our imagination. Something had hit us and then disappeared. The following week we were left questioning not only our senses but reality itself. We thought that at any minute the branches of a shrub would part and we'd see their childlike faces once again, and that when this happened everything would return to normal. But the children didn't appear, the police sweeps returned every day concealing their frustration, and each time we looked out at the jungle it seemed that the whole of it had turned against us in defense of the children. If this was no morality tale, we had to concede, it certainly looked like one.

Many years ago, reading a forgettable book, I came upon an image that entirely changed my understanding of reality. The author was describing a character who's looking out to sea and suddenly realizes that the word "sea" has never, in his mind, corresponded to the actual sea, that every time he's said "sea," he was thinking only of some outlandish foam-covered blue-green surface and never what the sea really *is:* a vast expanse full of fish, hidden currents and — especially — darkness. The sea is the true kingdom of darkness. The day the children disappeared, San Cristóbal residents felt something like this with respect to the jungle. Suddenly it seemed we'd confused the surface with the substance. In fleeing to its hidden depths, the children had taken us with them as if in a bathyscaphe. We may no longer have seen them, but we were closer than ever, inside their way of seeing, at the center of their fear.

Two months is a long time, and what happened in them remains a mystery to us. Anyone who finds it farfetched that the children survived with no help in such a hostile environment need only review the wild children of history — from the Hessian wolf children of the fourteenth century and the Bamberg boy who grew up among cattle in the late sixteenth century to Romulus and Remus, the mythical child patriarchs suckled by the Capitoline wolf. The hundreds of children who have survived, protected by Mother Nature or by animals, stand as undeniable human testaments. In 1923, in India, two girls were discovered — Amala and Kamala, aged six and four, raised by wolves in some part of Calcutta; in the mid-twentieth century Vicente Cuacua was raised in southern Chile by pumas; the Ukrainian girl Oxana Malaya was raised in the 1990s by dogs; and a community of green monkeys took in John Ssebunya in Uganda. Minimal research easily proves the existence of many similar, if not more astonishing, cases. There, in the lack of solemnity and the simplicity with which child and animal accept each other, begins the dialogue that the thirty-two undoubtedly had with the jungle, a dialogue that, it goes without saying, we were not party to.

As people, we are fascinated by anything that excludes us, but there's no guarantee that fascination yields logical thinking. The craziest ideas conceived and published about the thirty-two are, in point of fact, those dreamed up in those months. This is no coincidence: we start by projecting our own qualities onto anything we can't make sense of and end up believing that tigers fall in love, God is a jealous avenger and trees are nostalgic. Humankind systematically personifies anything it does not understand, from planets to atoms.

With regard to our great incomprehension of what happened in the jungle, we should reconcile ourselves to thinking more with scientific humility and less with authoritative arrogance. Why not contemplate the possibility — remote and fantastical as it might seem — that through those children nature was paving the way for a new civilization, a civilization unlike the one we defend with such unfathomable passion. Whenever I think like this, it transports me back to that time, to the way everything must have changed for those children deep in the jungle: light, time, who knows, perhaps even love.

It sounds almost like a story dreamed up by the same mind that entertained the sultan each night, thousands of years ago, so as to postpone her death one more day: a community of children locked in the heart of the jungle, abandoned to their fate, trying to invent the world anew beneath a canopy of leaves so thick that almost no light can penetrate. Jungle green is the true color of death. Not white, not black. The green that devours everything, an enormous, thirsty, mottled, stifling, powerful expanse in which the strong are sustained by the weak, the great steal the light from the small and only the microscopic and diminutive can stagger giants. The thirty-two survived in this jungle like a community of atavistic endurance. One day, as I hiked through one of the inland farms, I happened to rest my hand on a tree infested with a termite colony and had to snatch it back immediately. Hundreds of thousands of termites were devouring the inside of this fifteen-meter tree, giving off more heat than a furnace. The children's sense of community was similar to that of the insects: they were guests but also parasites; they appeared weak but were capable of destroying what had been the patient work of centuries. I don't want to fall into the very trap I've just condemned, but I could almost swear that this community of children abolished even love. Or a certain type of love. Ours.

We now know that one of the dead girls, a thirteen-year-old, was pregnant. There had to have been, therefore, relations among them, including among the younger children. Those months in the jungle must have been defining in that

sense. So how does love start from scratch? How does one
love in a world with no points of reference? The famous
Rochefoucauld maxim, that people would never have fallen
in love had they not heard it talked about, carries special
weight when applied to the thirty-two. Did they grunt, hold
hands, caress one another in the dark? What were their dec-
larations of love like, their longing glances? Where did the
rust end and the new begin? Perhaps, just as they invented
a new language based on Spanish, they took our timeworn
gestures of love as a start and turned them into something
else. At times I like to believe that we actually saw those gestures without comprehending them, that while they were in
the city their bursts of humanity occurred right before our
eyes. Something had been born at our expense, and in oppo-
sition to us. Childhood is stronger than fiction.

In that first month the police continued conducting sweeps of the jungle, albeit with ever-diminishing zeal. San Cristóbal had any number of problems and could ill afford to have a third of the local police force searching for a handful of kids, even if they had killed two people in the supermarket attack. In the suburbs alone there was a murder a week —all that year— and on the outskirts of the jungle there were known spots for drug trafficking and assaults. If that weren't enough, the supermarket episode led to an uptick in violence. That same weekend there were two holdups, one at a gas station and the other at the city's largest bank. The local police couldn't cope with it all, and the jungle was the closest thing imaginable to a prison of trees: the children were in there, they weren't going anywhere, and in all likelihood would come out when they got sick or hunger compelled them to do so. They were not the dilemma. The dilemma had started suddenly, someplace unanticipated: in our own children.

After the attack, parents began noting something strange about their kids. Bodies give off feelings, it's simply a matter of being close enough to perceive them, though it's not always easy to know what causes children's moods to change: a look they got from someone on Friday—sufficiently stewed over in their minds—might produce a crisis a week later. Prolonged silences, lack of appetite, withdrawal from activities that once brought joy—any of these responses might result from something totally banal or quite serious, and this ambivalence often leaves parents in a state of high alert that only those who have children can comprehend.

Had Teresa Otaño's diary not existed, we might have ended up forgetting all about this brief period of concern, but the written word stays with us; like photography, it too possesses the somber, granular persistence of evidence. After the supermarket attack, Teresa Otaño refers in her diary to Franziska, one of the fables that blends Ñeê tradition and

European folklore brought over by immigrants who settled here after World War II. Local anthropology seems to concur that the Ñeê version of Franziska is an amalgamation of the tale of Bicú, an old woman who steals other mothers' children because she cannot have her own, and Franziska, a Bavarian folktale bearing a certain similarity to the story of Aladdin.

The version told in San Cristóbal combines them like this: Franziska is born in a very humble home on the river Eré, everyone loves her so, and she has beautiful flaxen hair. After a number of rather trivial adventures, we learn of Franziska's secret power, albeit only indirectly. Far, far away lives a wizard who has spent years hunting for a treasure, and he discovers through a spell that a certain girl holds the secret he needs to discover the tree under which it is buried. This is where the most interesting part of the story comes, in the way the wizard decides to find Franziska: he puts his ear to the ground and, of all the sounds in the world, hears that of her footsteps as she's walking home through the jungle. I remember that in the early nineties in San Cristóbal, a famous storyteller, Margarita Matud, would tell this part of the story so well she left every child's mouth hanging open. She would climb up onstage dressed as a wizard and, with great flair, press an ear to the wooden floor. At this point a recording would be turned on, and out came the sounds of cars, conversations in multiple languages, drilling, trains and subways, footsteps both fast and slow, until finally the one thing that could be heard distinctly was the voice of a little girl on her way home. Is this not the best depiction of infatuation anyone could possibly imagine? The wizard's obsession with the girl renders all other sounds insignificant.

At some point, almost like a game, our children began putting their ears to the ground to listen for the thirty-two. A simple act, based on a story they knew well—the tale of Franziska. If the wizard could hear Franziska's footsteps from the other side of the world, why could they not hear the voices and footsteps of children only a few kilometers away? Whenever we walked out of the room, whenever they were left alone in the back garden, or between classes, or in their bedrooms, they crouched down, hearts pounding, and placed their ears to the ground, competing to see who'd be the first to hear the other children.

One afternoon I happened to walk into the bathroom abruptly and find my daughter, ear to the floor under the sink. Having no idea what she was doing there, I asked what she'd lost.

"Nothing," she replied, immediately blushing, her shame in turn causing me to blush. Whenever something like that happened I felt as if she'd grown up in a second, right before my eyes. She was only eleven, but tiny breasts had recently appeared, embarrassingly, beneath her shirt, and her hips had rounded out a bit. She looked less and less like Maia. Her character had changed as well. She no longer wanted me to walk her to school and had become more aloof, though she still blushed quite easily.

"Do you want me to help you?"

"No!" she cried, pushing me out of the way as she ran past.

Years later we—the adults—found a sort of explanation for these behaviors in Teresa Otaño's diary. It comes in the entries from early March 1995, when the street kids had been gone for approximately two months. Teresa explains it thus:

First you have to think of them. Hard. Try to imagine that their faces are really close to your face and you can almost smell their breath. With your eyes closed. Then you have to think about the things they think about and talk how they talk. In your mind. Because if you talk like them in your mind it's easier for them to understand you, because then they're doing the same as you, just someplace else. And you have to imagine you're not you, because you're not really in your body, you're above it, flying through the air. It's easy. Some people say there are magic words to say, but that's a lie. All you have to do is think really hard. That's what you do first. Oh, and you have to be alone, because they're alone too and they know so many more things than we do.

The first time I read the start of what is now referred

to as "the invocation of the thirty-two" I felt my blood run cold. For a second it was as if I were witnessing a ritual invented by a twelve-year-old girl, and I thought of how afraid my daughter must have felt when I found her in the bathroom that day. People often remark on the self-assured quality of the invocation, its instruction-manual tone, but I'd say that its intensity actually stems from what it dispenses with: adult logic, a world that no longer serves. How could our children possibly have explained to us what they were doing? We weren't prepared for their world or their logic. Somewhere out there, underground, that dissonant sound was being sent, in code: down below, chaos.

If you open your eyes by mistake you have to close them again and start all over, or else it doesn't work. Then you turn around three times until you're a little dizzy and get down and put your ear to the ground, but first pull your hair back. It's a little weird at first but then you get used to it. First you hear different sounds. Those are the sounds of the earth. The sound of ants and bugs. The sound of plants growing and people talking and breathing and cars driving past and the river going by and people walking. Then you start to think of something red. It's easy because your eyes are full of blood and if you put your face up to the light with your eyes closed you can see the blood in your eyes. Then it gets redder and redder and you think about it.

Seeing a child left to their own fear makes plain how

terrible the mind's attraction can be to whatever can destroy it. Whereas adults know that things will exist regardless of whether we take charge of them, children believe things will cease to exist if they don't keep them alive
in their thoughts. Teresa Otaño believes, without actually stating as much, that the Cat's existence is dependent
upon her thoughts, hence her sense of impotence and her
need to "cheat" with the invocation. She's distressed at the
thought of her memory fading, of no longer being able to
call to mind his features, his profile, the sound of his voice.
She wants to become him and thus keep him in the world.
There is, at this point in the invocation, a short digression.
Teresa writes about the Cat for a couple of paragraphs, says
that she wants the children to come back and mentions a
trip to the river that her father has planned for that weekend, saying she "hopes to see them." A moment later the invocation flies off in a wild direction.

The red is really red. Redder than the earth, as bright red as
volcano lava. And the sounds are fighting against the red and ev-
erything is fighting because you can hear the bugs and the noise
from the street but suddenly it's like there's a silence in the mid-
dle of all the red and that's when the children in the jungle ap-
pear and they're living in the trees. Then you have to think like
them, and thinking like them is the hardest thing in the world.
Because you're here and they're not. The red is what gets you

*there, like a car but with no sound. And then you think of all the
things that you have and they don't, and the things you can do
and they can't. Because they don't have a house. Or food. Or a
bed. And since they don't have those things they sleep with their
eyes open so they don't get scared. And they get inside you. And
you are them.*

Given that half the children of San Cristóbal had their ears to the ground in the hope of hearing the "jungle children" and the press was bombarding us daily with articles by psychotherapists about childhood fears, the groundwork had already been done by the time the Zapata children appeared. The first to speak of "telepathy" was Víctor Cobán, in a piece he wrote for *El Imparcial* published on February 7, 1995. He makes reference to a feature that had aired on local television two days earlier, when we saw the Zapata siblings for the first time. Three boys and a girl, ages five to nine, from the Candel neighborhood, they claimed to "paint" what the thirty-two *told them* in their dreams.

We've started to believe that our children can communicate with the jungle children, that they can speak to them, share dreams with them, even have the same visions. Plenty of thus-far sensible people are asking themselves: What next? A question that is perhaps not entirely well articulated. When a society starts to question everything, what we need to ask ourselves is not "Does telepathy exist?" but rather "Where do we hurt?"

But since surely neither Víctor Cobán nor any of us would have been capable of answering that question, instead we pondered telepathy. Believing in magic is the same as love: those convinced of its existence, and of falling in love, end up doing so sincerely, and those who doubt their feelings thwart the very possibility of having them, a paradox that leaves us forlorn, wondering what we might have become if only we'd allowed ourselves to believe. On the one hand, the Zapata children's drawings simply confirmed every stereotype that could be imagined about the thirty-two without knowing anything about them: huge gaping mouths inside of which were other, smaller mouths; children with swollen stomachs or dozing beneath a tree; blood; jungle foliage. On the other, they offered a new perspective, one as odd as it was plausible: things that seemed to be symbols, words with no apparent meaning that not even the Zapatas themselves could decipher, but which they swore they'd heard in their dreams; superimposed triangles, circles and suns with little planets around them. The Zapata children's artistic talent may not have been stellar, but this didn't mean they weren't convincing. The drawings were a strange cocktail, one part childish fantasy, one part sinister fear and one part invoked expectation. What made them hard to look at was not that they were any one of these things but that they were all three simultaneously.

It's been said many times that had the Zapata children been a little poorer or a little better-looking, had they been "too polished" or more eloquent, perhaps no one would have believed them, but these children possessed an extraordinary quality — that of normalcy. They were an assemblage of all things plausible. Born to a mother who taught high school and a father who worked in a bank, they looked like little fairy-tale elves. Friendly and well mannered, the boys and girl all responded to reporters' questions with a peculiar directness and huge, startled-looking eyes, perfect in a photo. One lisped. The eldest cued each of his siblings, like a perfect master of ceremonies. And the girl never stopped smiling. Each of their upper lips protruded slightly over the lower, giving them the appearance of poultry. Even before the feature story they'd garnered a certain fame in the neighborhood, and nearby families had begun visiting their home as though it were a place of pilgrimage. But it was

only after they were on the Maite Muñiz program that the
whole matter took on a truly public angle.

The TV-7 story aired on February 5, 1995, on the popular *At Home with Maite*. Local celebrity and presenter
Maite Muñiz was a woman of about fifty, with bleached-
blond hair, who embodied both the best and the worst of
San Cristóbal: she was sensitive and popular, but uncom-
promisingly shallow. Just as in all families there are members who are applauded and celebrated for the same reasons
that others are dismissed, in a relatively conservative city
like ours, Maite Muñiz's fame was the exception to the rule.
The three ex-husbands, the tax scandals, the racist comments she "didn't mean anything by," all were forgiven in
her case, thanks to her genuine likeability and unquestion-
able influence over public opinion. Oftentimes our greatest
defects are the direct result of our greatest virtues. Maite's
"cheek" and candor were poorly suited to the fundamental
structure of a daily program that required at least minimal
planning of its content. She had such self-confidence that
she far overestimated her ability to improvise on live television, which on more than one occasion had led to cuts and
personal grievances, some of which were quite infamous.
Once, for instance, she confused a little boy's name with that
of his disease, and another time she accidentally called the
ambassador to the Holy See "sweetheart" during his visit to
the region. People may have had to forgive Muñiz for cer-

tain things, the way they did a brazen family member, but she remained one of television's grandes dames.

The Zapata children's appearance on *At Home with Maite* was unexpected and hadn't been scripted, but when another story got dropped, an intern pitched the idea. Four hours later they were improvising a telecast from the family's home. First the camera pans the house, the patio, the slightly tacky way the parents have the children's drawings hanging from a sideboard in a sort of impromptu altar. Then the children emerge and Maite interviews them one by one, from the studio, asking simple, motherly questions. The children sometimes cut each other off and at other times finish one another's sentences as though they had rehearsed. "They tell us things with their minds," says the little girl. "At night," adds the lispy brother. A scriptwriter couldn't have come up with better lines.

"What do they say to you?"

"They say they're hungry," the eldest Zapata boy says unexpectedly.

The girl is the most affecting of the Zapatas. She holds her older brother's hand the whole time and is the only one of the four who seems slightly mischievous. From time to time she turns to her brothers and laughs quietly before turning back to the camera with solemn theatricality.

Fifteen minutes later, and entirely unscripted, Maite Muñiz improvises a now-famous monologue in which she claims that she *believes* these children, that the Zapata children are a bridge, a connection that could help us "mend our ways," and we must respond.

The episode has been ridiculed so often that people are reluctant to admit that the day it aired, we were all moved. It wasn't simply Muñiz's rather mawkish words (reproducing them here would do her no favors), but something we'd all been feeling inside and somehow resisted. Something still nameless, or something whose name was unpronounceable. And the program had enabled us to "feel" it. Perhaps expressing it this way sounds a bit ridiculous, but in truth what happened was scientific in its precision: Maite Muñiz acted as a conduit, channeling our desire for the children's return. I watched the program the next day, when they aired a rerun. All day I'd been hearing comments from everyone who had already watched the show, so when I got home I made sure to turn on the television. I managed to more or less maintain my composure through most of it, but, unsurprisingly, welled up when the eldest Zapata boy said, "They say they're hungry." I turned. The girl was on the sofa, her head in Maia's lap. We didn't dare look at one another. All three of us were moved.

It's also been said many times that the natural superstitious inclinations of the San Cristóbalites took care of the rest, but outsiders cannot fathom just how apt this was, or the degree to which white magic constitutes an actual form

of power throughout the region. A year before the altercations, the Department of Social Affairs conducted a statisti-
cal survey on white magic, and the results were astonishing:
four out of every ten people between the ages of twenty and
sixty claimed to have turned to it at least once in the space of
the preceding twelve months: spells, fortune-tellers, runes,
hexes. The evil eye is a San Cristóbalite's greatest fear bar
none, which says a lot about character. Often it's enough
for somebody to notice a person on the street looking at
them for more than a few seconds to make them seize up in
terror.

A few hours after *At Home with Maite* aired, dozens
of curious locals had already gathered outside the Zapata
house. Without intending to, Muñiz had articulated something in our conscience: *They're just children!* Children
who'd been forced to flee because of our animosity, children we'd treated like criminals, children we'd corralled
and whose deaths we might be responsible for at that very
instant. *Special children!* Beneath her layers of frivolity, she
had said the magic word, but the magic word, in addition
to raising our consciousness, also acted as a clarion call for
every witch in a hundred-kilometer radius.

The following week, the Zapata house was a veritable
hive of activity. Everybody wanted a taste of the honey. Everybody wanted to see the drawings, touch the children,
speak to the parents. Each time the four siblings appeared,

they looked increasingly compressed, as if they could no longer move an inch without touching. The Zapata kids were afraid, and their parents even more so. At one point, by popular demand, they opened the door to show people the children, and the throng stationed outside pounced so frantically they almost crushed the kids. People began bringing their sick to the house. City hall had to provide a police cordon to protect the home, a humble dwelling that clearly contained no valuables. But far from guaranteeing the family's safety, what resulted from our efforts was in fact the opposite: the deranged assumption that they were hiding something. The children couldn't go to school, and their parents were forced to take leave from work and hunker down for almost a week.

Twice the father came to the door to request respect for the family's privacy. "We haven't done anything to hurt anyone," he said rather absurdly, and then came back looking somewhat intimidated, but with a theatrical dignity, as though he wanted his expression to stop every one of those journalists in their tracks. "They don't know what they're doing," he declared.

On the eighth day the onlookers storm the house, forcing their way in. At two o'clock in the morning, fifteen people enter through a window and steal the children's drawings. A woman manages to snip off a lock of one of the boys' hair, no doubt for a magic spell, and on the way out some heartless bastard (who must already have known where the hiding place was) steals part of the family's savings, apparently kept in a box in the boys' room. The results of the incursion are broadcast on the local morning news. The father goes room to room, showing ransacked bedrooms, and says they've sent the children to stay with relatives for their own safety. Two hours later, it's the mother who summons the press to the door. With a dignity quite unlike her husband's, and as if it were the most normal thing in the world, she climbs onto a stool so as not to be steamrollered. Her breathing is agitated, but her tone is that of a teacher trying to calm a group of people she initially didn't take seriously and now fears.

She requests silence.

For several seconds the woman does not speak, waiting until the journalists finally grow quiet and all that can be heard is the sound of cicadas.

Then she drops the bomb.

"It was all a lie," she says. "I hope you understand, they were just being kids."

Loss of trust is similar to heartbreak. Both lay bare some internal wound, both make us feel older than we are. After the revelation of the Zapata children's lie, San Cristóbal became a tense place to live, a place where our children continued putting their ears to the ground, convinced that they would hear messages from the thirty-two, and we had begun to grow suspicious of what was quintessentially undeniable: their innocence. Of course, we'd have been incapable of expressing it in those words. We can only describe with any precision what we no longer feel, what we've somehow contained. The struggle to articulate feelings we're still experiencing is possibly the most touching, and useless, of them all. Perhaps that's why not even today, twenty years later, is it easy to communicate our loss.

The episodes that transpired over those months may have made us lose faith in the religion of childhood, but the children didn't have it much easier, and they certainly weren't waking up to a world any less hostile. For children, the world is a museum in which the adult guardians might be loving most of the time, but that doesn't stop them from imposing rules: everything there is solid, everything has always already existed, long before them. In exchange for love, the children are required to uphold the myth of their innocence. Not only do they have to be innocent, they have to perform it.

The Zapata case amounted to the expulsion of the children from our official religion. We had to punish someone, and since we couldn't punish our own kids, we decided to punish the thirty-two. Not only had they refused to act out the myth of Paradise Lost, they had begun to infect our own children. They were the black sheep, the slimy bruise that ends up rotting the fruit. Perhaps many people would find implausible such a blunt change in attitude: I would implore them to spend an afternoon in the archives, to verify

the change in tone reflected in the newspapers after the Zapata mother made her declaration.

And not just the newspapers.

According to the San Cristóbal Municipal Plenary Session minutes, item 3, Appeals and Requests, on February 13,
1995, Deputy Isabel Plante proposed for the first time that
the district's age of criminal responsibility be lowered. The
preliminary bill—drafted almost explicitly for the thirty-
two—attempted to abolish the provision of the Compre-
hensive Minors Act that stated, in the case of misdemeanor
or accessory to felony, any individual under the age of thirteen was exempt from imprisonment and would instead be
sentenced to custody overseen by civil commission. According to Madame Plante, the case of the "jungle children,"
as they were then being referred to, was so extraordinary
as to require its own specific legislation. She proposed special detention centers for any child under thirteen with no
known guardian who had taken part in the Dakota Supermarket attack, and conventional prison—the local penitentiary—for those over thirteen. In the event that this was
not approved by absolute majority (which would have been
required for the bill to be enacted), and knowing that the
bureaucratic process alone was going to take at least three
or four months, Madame Plante appealed to the urgency of
the circumstances and proposed the provisional creation of

a so-called Rehabilitation Board to reform the delinquent
youth who had already caused so much harm to the community of San Cristóbal and were now "rearming" (literally, her word) in the jungle for another attack.

The most disturbing thing was not that a conservative
deputy had proposed a draft bill that amounted to tram-
pling the most basic rights of a minor, but that 70 percent of
those present endorsed the proposal without so much as bat-
ting an eye. As liberal councilor Margarita Schneider said
many years later, referring to that time, "It was unbearably
odd . . . and yet it was bearable." We'd learned to use our
right hand to do things without the left finding out, which
allowed us to see not only that it wasn't so hard, but also that
we didn't actually feel so bad about it after all.

And yet our children kept on in their fantasies. Our
clear change of attitude, far from dissuading them, had
done the opposite: bolster their secret admiration. The
thirty-two had become their private place, the room they'd
decided we were not allowed to enter. I don't mean the
youngest children, who ultimately were as afraid as we
were, but those their same age, the boys and girls who
were nine to twelve years old. Something had divided
childhood into two.

In "Vigilance," the aforementioned essay on the altercations, Professor García Rivelles makes an interesting ob-

servation: "The dilemma about the supposed influence that the thirty-two had over San Cristóbal's children emerged in a way completely counter to what would have occurred in any traditional case of 'bad influence.' The thirty-two exerted their control from a *non-place*. Parents couldn't tell their kids not to behave like children they couldn't see, children who were not on the streets and who, to be fair, at that stage, none of us knew with any certainty were still alive. By not *being* anywhere in particular, the thirty-two had pulled off the unthinkable: they were everywhere. And thus, to any simple admonition that they not behave like those other children, the equally simple reply would have been: What children?"

That's the way things were. By losing their "realness," the thirty-two had morphed into the perfect monster, albeit one who exerted control more over the adults' nightmares than the children's. The thirty-two were the invulnerable void onto which the fascinating or the terrifying could be projected equally, a perfect screen. García Rivelles continues:

"The children of San Cristóbal intuitively saw that fantasy was the greatest virtue of the thirty-two. Was this an act of their own minds, or the adopting of an idea offered by the others? It makes no difference. In my view, it constitutes a true awakening. The power that the thirty-two had over the imagination of San Cristóbal's children was a supreme privilege and the source of their entitlements."

Or, to put it another way: *Your current freedom is the guarantee of our future freedom.* The children were free in the exact place where we were wounded—that of mistrust. When the time came, our children would assume the role of the thirty-two, not changing a thing: it was a matter of time; they were heirs. The shocking thing was that the deal had been made passively: the children of San Cristóbal seemed to assume the deaths perpetrated by the thirty-two, in some abrupt reversal of roles. Again, García Rivelles, this time in an almost Nietzschean tone:

"I made you, you made me; we're even. Or perhaps not. It's my blood that runs down your knife."

I don't think many people have dared to consider the altercations as freely as García Rivelles does in that essay. She proves herself capable of something near impossible: jettisoning all of the commonplaces that surround childhood so as to consider what happened in San Cristóbal in a new light, one that stems solely from the events themselves. But in order to expose a commonplace, one must first have experienced it, and in order to surpass it one must have employed it. The world of childhood was crushing us with its preconceived notions, which is why a large part of the irritation people felt for the thirty-two had less to do with whether it was natural for children to have perpetrated an act of violence than it did with the rage triggered by the fact that those very children had not confirmed their sugar-coated stereotypes of childhood.

Be that as it may, the worst was yet to come. Perhaps the greatest irony is that deep in our hearts we'd never stopped suspecting as much, not even for a minute.

Chronicles and narratives are like maps. On the one hand, you have the bold solid colors of the continents — collective episodes that everyone remembers — and on the other, the depths of private emotions, the oceans. It happened one Sunday afternoon, two or three weeks after the plenary session at which the Rehabilitation Board was created. Maia and the girl were both home. It was very hot, but this was the rainy season and our bodies had grown used to it. We felt bloated and moved in an oddly cadenced way, our muscles slack and our minds dazed. The sound of cicadas was deafening and, as it had rained early that morning, the humidity was stifling. We'd made pasta for lunch, and afternoon found us dozing in a post-Sunday-lunch melancholy.

When the doorbell rang I was on the verge of not answering it, but in the end I got up. Maia and the girl were asleep. I opened the front door to see a mestizo man of about my age, elegantly dressed and handsome despite how short he was. He conformed to the local standard of male beauty: clean-shaven, pointy-chinned. He asked for me, in a markedly San Cristóbal accent, and I told him that he'd found me.

"I'm Maia's father," he said.

It took me so long to react that he added:

"The girl's father."

It wasn't solely a question of the declaration being unexpected, it was the situation in and of itself. The features I loved in the girl, those same exact features, in this man were impersonal: small nose, brown smear for a mouth, dense eyes. And at the same time that his disjointed features were floating before me, I felt envious of them, as though I couldn't help but want them for myself. I asked him the most absurd question imaginable:

"Do you want money?"

The man stared back in shock, but also with the passivity so characteristic of San Cristóbalites that it makes them seem wise when in fact they are merely cautious.

"I wanted to speak to you."

I stepped out of the house and shut the door, and we walked two hundred meters in that sun to the riverwalk, without saying a word. My urge to get him away from the house was so great that I didn't stop to consider how ridiculous the whole situation was. I glanced sidelong at him a couple of times as he walked beside me. When I first met Maia I'd asked her repeatedly about the girl's father, but she'd always dodged my questions. Once when I'd insisted ad nauseam, she told me that as far as she was concerned he didn't exist, that she didn't even know where he was and that she wanted me to be the girl's father. For the first year we were married, the man's ghostlike presence caused me to suffer in silence, but in the end I gave in to the evidence that he had disappeared entirely. So what was he suddenly doing here? He wore white linen trousers and a short-sleeved shirt unbuttoned to the chest; he looked fashionable and purposeful, if a bit flashy—the sort of flashiness acceptable for a trader, not an affluent man. When we stopped by the river and I turned to look at him, I saw why Maia would have been attracted to this man. He was peaceful as a tree. I couldn't help but picture them together.

"I'm sorry to have bothered you," he said in a submissive

tone, and when I made no reply, he continued, "You're in charge of the children."

"You mean the jungle children?" The situation was so disconcerting I was unable to take in even the basic meaning of his words.

"One of them is my son."

It wasn't the first time something like this had happened. The images in the media after the Dakota Supermarket attack had led many families whose children had been missing for some time to convince themselves they'd identified the face of their son or daughter. Their understandable desperation made them believe, when there was no logical reason to believe. I myself had attended to some of those families and processed the documentation they brought us; many of them had been missing for years, and it took no more than a bit of arithmetic to realize it was impossible for these children to be the same age.

But this man was different. This man was like me. Worse, he was disconcerting, anonymous and yet absurdly familiar at the same time. The girl's face was contained within his, and Maia had slept with him, perhaps even loved him. He slipped a hand into his pocket and pulled out a leather wallet. Then he held out the photo of a boy of twelve, so like the girl it was stunning.

"His name is Antonio," he said, as though that settled everything. "You know where they are, don't you?"

"No, I don't. Nobody knows."

He eyed me distrustfully.

"I know he's with them."

The situation became instantly intolerable: the heat, my jealousy, the familiar tone he was taking with me. I felt cornered, rabid. As I turned to leave, he did something unanticipated. He grabbed the neck of my shirt, his expression heated, and said:

"You have to find him, do you hear me?"

All my life I've been a tranquil man, but on the few occasions I've experienced violence—as I did in that moment —it has always manifested as a burning sensation in my skull. Suddenly words sound different, thoughts become emotions, you stop understanding how you got there; it's like a feeling of dislocation. I shoved him so violently he nearly fell on his back. I was furious, but he was desperate. He sprung at me again and, because I didn't realize what he was trying to do, I threw a flustered punch that landed at the top of his left ear. It was like hitting a horse's flank and feeling the density of an animal's bone against my knuckles. He didn't even groan, simply straightened up, and with a humility that I couldn't understand at the time (though I do now: it was the humility required of desperation), he slipped into my pocket the photo of his son. As I tried to catch my breath, still in a daze, we stood in silence for a few moments, unsure of what to do. He touched his hand to his ear and then looked to see if there was blood; I leaned on the riverwalk railing and glanced around, afraid that someone had seen us. There was no one. The Eré flowed past, tons of water producing a muted sound. I was ashamed of having hit him. He had simple eyes, a simple nose, a simple mouth and chin. He was the girl's father. Now I knew I had nothing to fear. The man's desperation was like the river's presence, like the energy generated by that colossal mass carrying millions of tons of water and sand. He'd crossed some imposed limit. I intuited — I knew — that he and Maia had spoken at some point since our arrival in San Cristóbal and that Maia had forbidden him from approaching our house. I intuited — I knew — that, despite the fact that he may have wanted to see the girl, he must have rebuilt his life, and clearly had other children, Antonio among them. I wanted to ask him to forgive me but was unable to and took a step toward him. He didn't move.

"We're going to find them all . . ." I said, attempting to remember his name and realizing that in fact I didn't know it. He must have intuited this, because he said, "Antonio."

I walked back home slowly. I remember trying to return the photograph and him putting it back in my shirt pocket; I remember that in order to keep from looking at him, I fixed my gaze on an enormous leaf, the kind people call elephant ears, and that it seemed I could feel the soft, fleshy consciousness of the vegetation, the jungle that crept into the city again and again, as though awaiting the slightest opportunity to restake its territory. When I got home Maia was still asleep. She seemed younger than before, as young as when I'd first met her in Estepí. I lay down beside her and she opened her eyes upon feeling my weight on the mattress.

"You're sweating," she said. "Where were you?"

"Taking a walk."

That was all she asked. Reaching out her index finger, she wiped away a drop of sweat with her fingertip. For the first time, I thought that perhaps she'd made that same gesture with Antonio. That exact same gesture. And how many others. It seemed sad not to invent new gestures for each person we love, to have to carry around the same tedious gestures.

I was afraid that Maia would discover the boy's photo in my pocket and so took off my shirt, gazing at her all the while. She misinterpreted the move and took off hers. Playing along with the misunderstanding, I got all the way undressed. She did the same. Despite her age, Maia had a childlike appearance: small breasts, a body with almost no hips, like a boy. When she was naked it was as if any part of her body could look out. Her stomach often palpitated.

I entered her with a kind of harshness, kissing her neck to keep her from looking at me. I could feel something perverse inside of me, as though what excited me was the

fact that I knew she'd spoken to Antonio behind my back.
We knew each other so well, knew how to find each other,
knew one another's curves and angles. It was clear that we
intended to be quick and efficient. And we were. But I also
felt a desperation in her, something less habitual: in the
middle of our familiar choreography, she held me tightly,
and for a second I thought she was trembling. Then she lay
her chin on my shoulder and whispered that she loved me.

After we finished, we lay staring up at the ceiling fan.
It seemed we had so many things to talk about, and at the
same time nothing to say. Perhaps one of the greatest sur-
prises about marriage is precisely that: the inevitable for-
mality, even when you know the other's body and habits
better than your own. Light filtered in through the blinds'
slats and projected a curve beneath her nose, a sort of smile.
I once again marveled at the inscrutability of my wife's face.

"Do you regret having married me?" I asked.

I had never asked anything even remotely along these
lines. It was one of those flawed questions, born of simple
egotism and insecurity. I'd always managed to avoid them,
but for some reason this time was unable. I was wounded.

"You are my love."

"That doesn't answer the question," I prodded.

She smiled. A fragile smile, like heartache, an involuntary gesture.

"Of course it does," she said.

I think about those weeks and all I see is that boy's face. I've still got the photograph, but for some reason his image looks different there than in my memory. And it's that imagined face (as opposed to the photograph: an ordinary boy with a furrowed chin) that comes to mind when I close my eyes. His face is an oval, like the girl's. Their features are similar too, though on him they look bolder, as if what's still veiled in the girl, in the boy has already taken on a pre-adolescent air.

When I looked for him in the video footage from the supermarket I spotted him instantly. He was slightly shorter than the others and had a distinct haircut, straight across the middle of his forehead, like a bowl. It could only be him. He was one of the first to walk in, and also one of the killers. At a certain point, he approached Feni Martínez (one of the victims) with staggering nonchalance and plunged a carving knife into her stomach, three times. Then he froze, watching as she collapsed and bled out on the floor. Unlike the second murder committed during the attack, the one perpetrated by Antonio Lara does not look like a game; there's a horror to it that does not fade. It's almost ceremonial, studied. He stands looking at his victim for several seconds and then crouches down to observe her from up close, or perhaps to tell her something. At the last second, the two of them take the measure of each other with their eyes. The boy reaches out a hand but does not touch her. It has a sinister feel, this gesture. Twisted and yet utterly childlike.

The image of Antonio occupies the entirety of my memory of those weeks. The physical image, the mental image, as though the one fed off the other via some internal channel, growing more engorged each day. I couldn't look at the girl without seeing him hovering over her every expression. I felt as if at any moment blood would out, that she'd put an ear to the ground or close her eyes and hear his voice in her dreams, like the Zapata kids had. Perhaps the Zapatas hadn't been lying. Perhaps it was true after all and there was some tremendous flow of dreams and thoughts coming from the jungle into our homes.

When I was alone in my office at city hall, I would take out the boy's photo and hold it beside the one of Maia and the girl. Together they had a strange power, a static charge. I'd seek out the girl when I got home, more desperately than I normally might, and she would avoid me. This was painful, but I would tell myself she was on the brink of becoming a young woman and that withdrawal was normal at her age. I understood, and yet for some reason everything made me uneasy. I saw signs everywhere: in the girl, on the street, in the heat, even in positive things—Maia's affability, the river's beauty, the empty silence every time the cicadas in the jungle stopped singing.

Maia, at the time, was practicing Sibelius's Violin Concerto, one of the most beautiful pieces I ever heard her play. She was confident about making first violin in a local orchestra, but her ambition got the better of her and the piece slightly exceeded her abilities; it was too rigorous, the melody's phrases so precise that one tiny error would throw the sense of the whole composition into disarray. I watched her attempt it over and over, a piece that almost no one was going to understand, and it seemed to me that the phrasing of the score was getting under her skin. Sibelius's melody was like a network of veins, simple and unwavering like a cascade of pressures, diminutive expressions.

That was when it started happening. When the children started disappearing. Our children. At first no one believed it, they seemed like isolated cases, unrelated. It was assumed that sooner or later they'd reappear, that the police would phone from some gas station, holding the kids by the hand, or that someone would see them in front of somebody's house and notify the local officials, but the hours ticked by with an agonizing quality. We'd have preferred a kidnapper. A murderer even. Any kind of horror we were familiar with. The first case took place on March 6, Alejandro Míguez, nine years old, son of a cardiologist and a post office worker; the second, two days later, Martina Castro, daughter of a couple employed by city hall's cleaning service; the third, Pablo Flores, eleven years old, son of a young widower, a financial columnist at *El Imparcial*.

They disappeared between March 6 and 10, 1995. Looking back now at the local press coverage from that period is almost infuriating. The articles talk of the children's disappearances and next to the photos report news on child mafias and express kidnappings. Their silence about the thirty-two serves as the perfect barometer for the degree to which we avoided all mention of what we dared not think about. Even Víctor Cobán seemed unnerved and wrote a column full of banalities on the dangers of allowing our children to roam freely, as we did back then, as though the only problem were not holding their hands while crossing the street or letting them play unsupervised in parks across the street from our houses.

What must it take for three well-raised, middle-class kids with no significant family trouble — some of them anxious by nature, if we're to believe their parents' testimony — to run away from home, sneak out a window or crawl under the shrubbery, in order to join the pack of kids hiding out in the jungle? Even assuming we managed to find out how they succeeded in contacting them, what led them to run away? What electric current jumped from those children to ours? The kids who didn't succeed in joining them — the ones who were caught in flagrante with a foot out the window, ready to flee — were themselves unable to explain it very well. On being interrogated they started crying, obfuscated, as if the question were so vicious that it outweighed whatever had led them to try to run away to begin with. They said they wanted to be with their friends, but when asked *what* friends, they described places and situations that would have made it impossible to reach them.

Also much commented on at the time were certain episodes, filmed by cameras in commercial establishments and private homes alike, in which the children appear, always at night. Several instances of food theft were verified, and all indications point to it having been them, but of all the images included by Valeria Danas in her biased documentary *The Kids,* only one comes from that particular week: a home video taken by a frightened father in which a group of four can be seen jumping the fence at a house and then speaking to a boy leaning out a window. The image has the graininess of night: first a group of kids is seen with their little noses raised to the window, clustered together so tightly it's as if they were a single being; then the beguiled boy, in the solitude of a king.

Each time I see this image I try to recall the strategies children use to beguile, the ones I'd observed in the girl in the early days, when I'd take her to the park in Estepí — the always clumsy formulaic routine, the approach and withdrawal; the risk of exposure and the beauty of triumph over another's will; the feeling, so hard to communicate but so easy to see, that one has gotten the other's attention. The dialectic of seduction, in children, is much more instinctive than it is in adults; it's set to a different temperature, possesses a different logic, and, of course, a different violence.

In this nighttime video, you can see the boy leaning out the window gradually stop feeling afraid. A sequence of facial expressions confirms this, and then a silly face that seems to be a smile, as though the group of kids has hit upon something both amusing and convincing. The boy at the window disappears and returns a few minutes later with several cans, but the conversation doesn't end here. He leans over and touches their hair, first one and then another, who is taller than the others and turns out to be a girl. A beautiful girl with a tangle of stringy hair, a miniature lion. I've likely watched this footage more than twenty times and in very different situations, but only recently did it strike me how few words are exchanged. How little the children speak. A silent seduction. I wish my wife were alive so that I could ask her why something as simple as this rattles me so.

Until the tenth of March, the city of San Cristóbal limited itself, with respect to the disappearances, to the same reaction it had always shown when cornered: suffer in silence until the problem fades away. But the opposite happened. On March 10, the front page of *El Imparcial* included a call to arms by Pablo Flores—father of one of the disappeared children—in which he urged the entire city to convene in Plaza Casado at eight o'clock that night. The summons (which, being a columnist at the paper, he'd managed to publish in the metro news section) attempted to persuade the populace to take up the fight, "given the unforgivable negligence on the part of the police and their inability to find our children." Pablo Flores's call had the electric charge of a manifesto. It began with a direct, second-person appeal to all San Cristóbal residents: "Look at your son, at your daughter . . ." Then he named that which had been supremely unnamable: "Ever since the Dakota Supermarket attack, people in this city are afraid even to say the word 'child.'" Flores got to the heart of the matter like an expert: "With every minute that goes by, every second, it becomes a little bit harder to find my son." He signed off with an aggrieved plea: "Help me."

Even now it's hard to know exactly what Pablo Flores expected when he issued that open call to meet in Plaza Casado. Most likely (as with Antonio Lara when he'd grabbed me by the collar at the riverwalk a week earlier) it was the simple desperation of an anguished father, but Flores far exceeded the typical profile of a rabble-rouser. An economist by training, forty-three years old and recently widowed, he had returned to San Cristóbal after working in the capital for a decade and was cut from a familiar cloth, that of the highly qualified professional. Clearly, things had not gone well. A few months after his return, a sudden heart attack had ended his wife's life, and a year later, when he was beginning to get over her death, his son had disappeared without the slightest trace.

The same day that the public notice appeared in *El Imparcial* — and on seeing how close the situation was to spinning out of control — Mayor Juan Manuel Sosa convened a crisis cabinet and proposed banning the demonstration, at which "anything could happen." The mayor was afraid —and rightly so—of becoming not only the man politically responsible for everything that had happened since the

Dakota attack but also the perfect target for people's rage. Put in perspective, the meeting could have served as a master class in provincial politics: not only was there a populist mayor accustomed to acting like a cacique, but also an entourage of handpicked officials set against a backdrop of the people's unsustainable rage.

Juan Manuel Sosa's chief defect, like that of most provincial politicians, was not malevolence but lack of imagination. To a man like him, Pablo Flores was the quintessential antagonist: still young, talented and class-conscious. Not only was the man a natural enemy, he was also keeping a steady eye on the mayor and threatening him with a deadly stone: the negligence with which he'd handled the entire children's crisis. Someone suggested that, far from banning the Plaza Casado demonstration, the mayor should participate in an institutional capacity, so as not to be identified as the "official enemy." The situation was so desperate and the parents so anxious to find their children that any political danger posed by the situation would be defused the moment the people saw clear signs and expressions of apology.

And, against all predictions, at eight o'clock that night, facing a rabid crowd, Sosa climbed up to the podium at which those angling to defenestrate him were scheduled to speak. I could never have imagined the outcome. What happened, I suppose, was that the politician in him came out. He may truly have believed it could all be fixed by a couple of bear hugs and some photos of him kissing kids, but nobody thought to give him a hug and there were no kids there to kiss. The whistling and booing were so loud that his smile froze the moment he got to the stage. One person made as if to hurl a bottle, and for a second you could see the terror on his face, but he quickly regained composure. After all, of the more than four hundred people who attended, thirty were plainclothes police officers forming a human shield to keep him from being lynched.

I stood watching from the back of the plaza. The crowd seemed to be swept up in a kind of energy that incited them, which is why it seems almost miraculous that violence didn't break out sooner than it did. The mayor's speech was so preposterous that it enraged people still further; far from averring that the city's police were already looking for the children, he exculpated himself in pathetic fashion and assured everyone that from that moment on he personally would see to the matter (thus giving the opposite impression—that until that moment he had not done so).

It was at this point that Pablo Flores climbed onstage and shouted, "We have to find our children!" and a roar erupted in Plaza Casado that still shakes me to recall. Considering the peaceful if not dumbstruck nature of most of the individuals there, it seems impossible that their reaction was so sudden. In the footage recorded by Valeria Danas, the sequence is interrupted shortly after that roar of approval, but in real life it went on for five long minutes. Five minutes of applause and shouting. It was as though the duration changed the very nature of the uproar: it began as approval, then who knows what it was. Threat. Rage. The mayor exited the stage quickly. I thought we were in danger. All of us, everyone there — in danger. Pablo Flores himself looked semi-hysterical, his eyes red with desperation and no doubt lack of sleep after three days of fruitless searching. Nothing is more dangerous than the insanity of inherently sane men. Unlike the naturally violent man, the sane man's violence has a radical, helpless character. Had anyone put Pablo Flores's son before him at that instant, he may not have recognized him, distress had so clouded his vision.

There was little else he could say. At one corner of the plaza — the one closest to the stage — a fight broke out. The sound on the mike went out. For a few moments it seemed as if things were going to die down, and then out of nowhere the fight turned into a pitched battle. More than thirty people were suddenly involved in a brawl surely provoked by the undercover officers protecting the mayor. The police detail waiting at the edge of the plaza, prepared for any possible altercation, intervened immediately and exacerbated the situation irreversibly.

Fifteen meters from where I stood, I saw Antonio Lara's easily recognizable neck and tried to approach, but soon lost sight of him. I got out of there as best I could and headed for city hall. Half an hour later I learned that the fight had resulted in twelve injured, none critically, and three arrests, including that of Pablo Flores. I also learned something else: during the fracas that night, three more children had disappeared—two boys and a girl—all of them taking advantage of the commotion in Plaza Casado.

Love and fear have one thing in common: they are both states in which we allow ourselves to be fooled and guided, we entrust another person to control our beliefs and, what's more, our destiny. I've often wondered how the crisis of the thirty-two would have been handled if it had taken place just ten or fifteen years later. The chasm between January 1995 and January 2005 (or 2010) would be irreconcilable. Truth, the superficial spectacle of truth, social media and a few cell phones that can turn a ninety-year-old woman into a reporter, none of this existed in the not-too-distant—and yet astonishingly faraway—year of 1995. The mere meaning of the phrase "This is real" has changed more in the past two decades than in the past two centuries, and the Eré riverwalk on which San Cristóbalites now stroll and snap photos of themselves at dusk is both the same place and an utterly different one. It's been changed by something more mysterious than the passage of time: the suspension of our belief. Did all of those things really happen? Young people hear the story as if it were some mythical fable, and we—those who saw it unfold with our own eyes—don't seem much more convinced. The pictures, ultimately, don't serve for much after all. Having seen the corpses of the thirty-two laid out along the riverwalk has not added a great deal.

I now know that on the night of the demonstration in Plaza Casado part of me stopped being the person I'd been all my life. I returned to city hall as slowly as possible, my body still shaken, trying to devise a plan. A strange determination came over me, and when I arrived I went straight to Juan Manuel Sosa's office. He was in a meeting with Amadeo Roque and kept me waiting for over fifteen minutes. As I sat in the little vestibule outside his office, my determination took shape, in a detached sort of way.

They called me in. The secretary closed the door. The air in the room was charged. This was the first time I'd been alone with Juan Manuel Sosa in his office. It was as though

I could perceive his distress and that feeling of imminence people always give off when they're afraid. Only then did I realize that he was furious at his Plaza Casado humiliation. For a reason I can no longer recall he was convinced that I had been one of the ones to promote the idea of his appearance before the crowd. He asked me who I thought I was. For a moment it looked as if he was going to get up and lunge at me, but instead he simply gripped the armrests of his chair in an oddly delicate way. More incongruous still was my own reaction: I asked coldly what on earth he'd thought was going to happen. I told him that he had no friends and that nobody at city hall spoke plainly to him. Even as I spoke those words, I wondered what was leading me to such suicidal action, a question that remains a mystery to me. I realized that many of the things I was about to do were reproachable and even actionable, but congratulated myself for having come up with a quick solution beneficial to all: it avoided a popular uprising and put us in a good position to end the crisis.

I told him my plan: manipulate the press, supplying them with an official version of events to reduce the possibility of an uprising the following day, and get Pablo Flores out of lockup and send a search party into the jungle at dawn, a search party comprised of *absolutely every* police reserve in the city. We had to find the children. Immediately. It would be enough—I told him—to find one. Children are not adults, I said, "children will talk, you simply have to know how to make them."

The mayor asked me what I meant.

I said I didn't think it was necessary to explain.

There came a silence and again he stroked the armrests of his chair. Night had fallen, and we sat in the darkness of that room like two bats. He turned on a light and asked me my name. It was then that I realized that until this point I'd been speaking to someone totally divorced from the most basic understanding of reality. He hadn't recognized me but was staring at me the way a drunkard stares at the wife he despises—with a twisted, belligerent sneer. He demanded that I spell out my plan, and I did so. You could almost hear his crude but efficient brain begin to work.

"If I go down, you go down," he said finally, and when I didn't respond right away, added, "If I go down, you all go down."

I tried to concentrate on his face, shocked to have so imprudently tied my fate to this political corpse.

"So it seems," I replied.

"If I go down, you all go down."

In certain situations, what one is supposed to feel is so obvious that not to feel it seems unreal. The reasons for this don't dull the pain, but they do explain it; the urgency of what's real fades and there appears a halo of fictionality, as though someone else has made the decision on our behalf. I see the image of myself there before the mayor, and it's as if it were some other person, external and foreign. I remember what I looked like at the time, but the feeling that led me to speak those words (with all of their implicit violence) is intact; it looks like me, but there is something perverse and distorted inside it, as though suddenly I went to blink, and my eyelids had been turned inside out.

Other times I'm more reasonable—more indulgent, perhaps—and think that the whole performance was akin to a very common occurrence: a boy testing his father over the course of several days until finally the father loses patience. There comes the moment of blind rage when he slams a hand down on the table and rises to punish his son, the second prior to physical violence when it is only *mental* violence. Is something not at stake in that moment? And the expression on the child's face as he turns toward his father and realizes that he's crossed the line—is it real or still just looming, something yet to happen, something not yet real? The thirty-two had crossed that line, and the city of San Cristóbal had slammed a hand on the table, but between rage and real violence there was still some distance.

It didn't take much to bribe Manuel Ribero, editor of *El Imparcial*. All I did was follow the instructions Sosa had given me. I said that I was speaking on the mayor's behalf and that the following day he was not to publish a single word about the last three children to disappear or the fight that had broken out in Plaza Casado if he wanted the city to keep the contract that enabled the paper to make its crippling loan payments. There came a sad and ominous silence that led me to suspect this was not the first time a comparable scene had played out, albeit with different actors. Again my composure surprised me.

"We don't want a popular revolt on our hands," I continued. "We have to focus on the search for the children and must not compromise their *safety*."

Safety, that magic word, an invocation capable of suspending the most basic logic. Manuel Ribero took some time in responding. He told me he would agree not to print anything about the most recent disappearances but that it was impossible not to publish what had happened in the plaza: there were too many witnesses, and he already had a staff writer assigned to the piece. I told him to turn the piece into a letter to the editor, that the paper's official position was to be that the event at Plaza Casado had transpired with utmost normalcy, that I myself would write the piece and send it to him in an hour.

It's surprising how quickly and efficiently people buckle when confronted with abusive behavior in crisis situations. This was the first (and last) time I had bribed anyone in my life. I'd anticipated feeling Manuel Ribero's resistance as well as my own disgust, and although both of these did occur, the particular urgency of the situation, what led him to accept and me to bribe, was manifestly *outside* the expected framework. At no point did I think we'd both feel the same unanticipated and almost simultaneous fear—as though the bribing of one and the humiliation of the other constituted some sort of common ground—and certainly not that this fear would unite us in such an odd way, as if an involuntary response were protecting us both. A private act.

I asked him if he had children. He told me three.

"There is nothing pleasant about this," he said.

"But it won't go on much longer," I replied.

"It will go on as long as people like you and me keeping doing things like this."

That was a discreet lesson. One that took me some time to understand, because the urgency of that night would never have let me see that what he said was no personal attack; I took it as such and responded with arrogance. He said nothing more, simply hung up the phone and has not spoken to me since. Twenty years have gone by since that night, and each time I've run into him and tried to approach, he has very clearly turned his back. Had he let me speak on any of those occasions for even half a minute, he'd have known that all I wanted was to thank him for that remark.

The sweep was set for five o'clock the following morning, March 11, 1995. In addition to 164 municipal and provincial police officers, we were expecting at least 40 volunteers, the majority being relatives of the children who'd most recently disappeared. Pablo Flores was the one who conscripted them. We needed someone who was seen, in the eyes of the families, as an authority figure, and who better than Flores? We gave him a short list of instructions for anyone wanting to sign up and told him punctuality was of the essence. I hardly slept that night, only leaving my office at two in the morning once I'd made sure that *El Imparcial* was going to publish the piece I'd written about the Plaza Casado incident.

Before going home, I stopped in to see Amadeo Roque, the chief of police, who was in his office meeting with his team to plan the route for the dawn sweep. Contrary to what many believe, Roque was basically a good guy. Irritating and thin-skinned, to be sure, but ultimately a good guy. His dour face and incipient hair loss were poorly suited to his wide, almost feminine hips, but he'd learned to make up for it by always moving briskly. With him were four other people, bent over a large map of the outskirts of town. Roque was speaking somewhat louder than usual, and his team looked slightly cowed. To me it seemed that the entire affair had overwhelmed him to an anxiety-producing degree; it was as though the unpredictability of what might happen had caused a short circuit in the strict logic he used to process his thoughts. It wasn't just that he'd had his knuckles rapped more than a dozen times by the mayor, or that his job was on the line; this was deeper, more fundamental—something he was having a hard time relating to, something that was making him rashly overreact to trivial stimuli.

We were all exhausted, with a living-dead sort of air about us. Amadeo Roque had tried to mark the point on the map where the first group was to begin the next day, but his pencil lead broke and, rather than sharpen it or ask for another, he snapped the pencil in two and threw it in his assistant's face. It was an odd moment, unexpected, particularly in a man like him, who worried neurotically about how his actions were perceived. More than a violent reaction, it was like a performance, or the rehearsal for a performance. Like he wanted to see himself doing something unpredictable. I now realize he was not the only one. Everyone at that meeting was treating each other with oblique detachment, not so much because we couldn't predict one another's reactions as because we were losing control of our own.

Two hours later there was no one at city hall. We'd left almost without saying goodbye. It seemed paradoxical how calm a night it was, given everything that had transpired. The moon was nearly full and the trees cast shadows on the many sections of sidewalk where there were no streetlights. On the fifteen-minute walk home it struck me that a child could jump out at me at any moment. I pictured him with a hunched back and the face of Antonio Lara, in the photo his father had given me, which I carried with me always. In my imagination he looked like one of those mythical creatures from children's fables—a goblin or an elf. For a few minutes, as in the fables, I thought his appearance depended solely on my wishing it so, and that if I wished hard enough the boy would eventually appear. But wish I did, and no one appeared. There was only the slightest of breezes, and everything was still when I got to the front door. There were no lights on in the living room or in the girl's room, and only a faint one in the bedroom coming from Maia's nightstand.

Opening the front door, I was greeted by Moira, the dog I'd hit on the way to our new house the day we first moved to this city. We had not succeeded in turning her into a family pet. She would spend long stretches of time with us but then disappear for months, returning half starved or with her neck torn up from a fight. The dog had understood that our house, more than a home, was a center she returned to in the hope of a miracle. Each time she came we welcomed her joyfully, but also uneasily. Maia refused to touch her, out of superstition, and we'd forbidden the girl from playing with her, for fear of the germs she brought back each time she came. That last time she'd been even closer to death than the day she'd been hit: a tropical blowfly had inserted its larvae under her skin, and the maggots had been feeding off her flesh for so many months that by the time she came back to us she was almost a lost cause. I'd parted the fur on her neck with my fingers to discover, with inexpressible revulsion, a wriggling ball of maggots the size of a mandarin orange. This seething mass of blind larvae had gone still for a split second and then started writhing even more furiously. Now the dog was okay again. She panted energetically and stared at me in the darkness with an intensity that in a human would have been unbearable. Her wound had healed and all that remained was a bald patch under her collar.

Everything fights death, I thought, from maggots to sequoias, from the river Eré to a termite. I will not die, I will not die, I will not die; this seems to be the one true cry on the planet, the one genuinely undeniable force. It was proven by Moira the dog, wagging her tail at me when I arrived, by the girl sleeping in her room, by the attention Maia paid to me as I recounted what had happened when I walked into the bedroom, by the intense flicker of intelligence in my wife's eyes. And as I spoke, I experienced a fervent need for that primeval cry — I will not die, I will not die, I will not die — and got the feeling that something passed over us, over Maia and me, something like a magic spell. But not even its benevolent energy could quell the anxious cry.

I described the Plaza Casado fight in detail.

I told her that I'd bribed the editor of *El Imparcial* that night, and that at dawn the sweep would begin, and that we were determined to put an end to the whole matter once and for all.

Maia told me to close my eyes and try to rest. I looked at her without saying anything. There in the darkness, the pupils of her black eyes were enormous, like those of a newborn. I felt that in some unspeakable way she was proud of me, but for reasons that were far from clear and which, as always, she had no intention of sharing with me. Suddenly I was overcome by the exhaustion of the day, but the more silent things around me became, the louder that implacable cry. Lying on her side next to me, Maia put a hand on my back. A simple gesture, something she did whenever she wanted to calm me. The same small, warm hand as always, fingertips rough from violin strings, but now it felt hot, as though rather than a hand it were something harsh, a poker someone was using to nudge me, little by little, toward a cliff. And all the while that cry could be heard again and again, sometimes with the harsh wheeze of a cackle and others mellifluous and unsettling. I will not die, I will not die, I will not die . . .

I awoke covered in sweat.

"You've been talking in your sleep this whole time," Maia whispered.

"What was I saying?"

"I couldn't quite understand."

"You don't want to tell me?" I asked.

My wife had an odd way of avoiding requests she didn't like: she smiled and shot to kill.

"If you don't want to know, why ask?"

Our conversations often ended in this way, like some Eastern fable. I told her that I might not be back that night; the idea was to continue the sweep until we'd found the children. She told me not to bear the weight of a situation that was beyond my control. She also said something troubling, something very Maia: not to be afraid.

"Afraid of what?" I asked.

"Of finding them."

At five o'clock in the morning the air had a crystalline quality, a few streetlights were still on, and not a single sound could be heard. I was so tired that until I'd gone two hundred meters toward the riverwalk, I didn't realize that Moira was trotting along beside me. She was wearing her white parasite collar, which had a little bell that tinkled softly every time she moved. Again I found myself amazed, as I had the first time I saw her, by the elegance of her shepherd mix. I realized that she was trying to return some sort of favor and patted her head in appreciation.

The group was comprised of more than two hundred people, including police and volunteers. Everyone had gathered at the tourist pier. I was surprised that there were so many people, that they were so willing. The pier at that time bore little resemblance to the one here today, and the boat that used to do river crossings back then was nothing like the brand-new white catamaran everyone in San Cristóbal is now so proud of; it was a blue tub that some joker had christened *Mestizo*. Amadeo Roque climbed on deck and shouted through a megaphone that he was the chief of police and was going to give instructions on how to carry out a sweep. He looked marginally less exhausted than he had the night before, but also more tense. He was gripping the taffrail so tightly it looked like he was taming a wild horse. Roque shouted that on this first day the sweep was to go almost six kilometers into the jungle, that it was impossible for the kids to have gotten any farther than that. The idea was to begin on the eastern side—the last place to have had several child sightings—and from there fan out to the west of the city, like a circular hunting group.

The men (the party was made up almost entirely of men, the only exceptions being five or six women who at the time worked in law enforcement) were nervous. In general, they had followed the instructions we'd given them: to wear long pants and boots and light cotton clothing. They looked both stern and sleepy. For a second, the scene reminded me of the middle-of-the-night pilgrimages we went on when I was a boy, to commemorate the arrival of spring. A rite as ancient as humankind: celebrating the cycles of life, marking the change of seasons, asking the gods for prosperity. Compared to the bipolar jungle, which had only the dry and the rainy, the world of actual seasons seemed a galaxy away. Amadeo Roque shouted instructions from the rear, and in the dawn light his features, blurry until that moment, became distinct. One of the groups in the sweep, the one closest to the river, was being led by Pablo Flores. Giving him a degree of authority in the operation had definitely been the right choice. His anxiety seemed to have come slightly undone—no doubt due to exhaustion—though he still had the same crazed expression he'd worn when climbing onstage in Plaza Casado. Antonio Lara, however, I could not see. I knew for a fact that he was in the group, as I'd noticed his name on the list, but I couldn't find him. Three whistles sounded. This was the signal to begin the sweep, and we got into position.

We'd learned from the failure of our first sweep, after the Dakota Supermarket attack. This time every man carried a machete, a whistle and a flashlight, and for every ten people there was a snakebite kit—prepared by the health department the previous night—with antivenom for every kind of snake in the province. They'd drawn up a poster so people would know how to tell a python from a rattler or a coral snake, and the antivenom had been placed in colored vials with pictures of the corresponding snake's head on each one. Almost as important as injecting the antivenom as fast as possible, one of the doctors on the sweep explained, is knowing what kind of snake bit you, and he gave a short demonstration of how to inject the antivenom, first pinching your skin up. A syringe of antihistamine was provided as well, in case of spider bites. The chief of police insisted on the importance of keeping a twenty-meter distance between people, and of never losing visual contact with the people on either side of you. If anyone saw a child, they were not to give chase but simply to use the whistle and keep approaching at the same speed, not breaking the cordon *no matter what*.

A good part of people's memories depends on the way feelings and impressions affect them over time. Was the air really such a milky white when we entered the jungle, or was that a mere distortion of my feelings? I was very familiar with the first stretch of the jungle, the part by the river. When I was new to the city there were popular picnic spots there, and I used to take Maia and the girl. Those areas were still there, albeit now derelict. The grills had been removed, but the remains of the brick tables still stood, like primitive ruins of an ancient civilization. It seemed a thousand years had gone by since then, and I longed for my old naïve self. But trees have no interest in good and evil, insects and plant roots have no interest in the reasons of man, much less his longing, and there is something comforting about that.

It was almost like a game: a clear line of people disappearing into the dense foliage, forging a path with machetes but as stealthily as possible. The only sounds were those of our slow footsteps, avoiding—as we'd been told to do—branches and fallen trees, and from time to time a whistle in the distance. One whistle meant stop; two, resume the sweep; three, that one of the kids had been found. In the case of three whistles we were to head for wherever it had come from, maintaining the distance between the men on either side of us in order to loop around, surrounding the group. We were walking slowly, so slowly that after just a few minutes we'd almost lost sense of which direction to go. In addition to that, on crossing a small tributary of the Eré we had to regroup and then fan out all over again. We wasted nearly an hour and a half on this simple procedure before managing to reestablish our positions. People seemed absorbed, silent. Over two hours of trudging through deep jungle can bring on a state of glazed melancholia, and I've always thought that a good part of the Ñeê community's solemnity stems from the inevitable slowness that vegetation imposes on people's thoughts. But we were all sure of one thing: we were going to find those children. It might take a few hours or more than three days, but sooner or later we were going to find them. And as odd as it seems, Maia was right: that idea frightened us.

The dog trotted easily beside me; she seemed very familiar with the area and only occasionally did she run a few meters off to sniff some tree trunk, always returning with a scowl. I thought she had no idea what I was looking for, but at one point she stopped short and growled purposefully. I looked in the direction Moira stared and saw nothing. A wall of vegetation, a mass of trees and bare red earth.

Sunlight had begun to filter through the highest leaves of the tree canopy, flecking the ground with bright spots. The intuition wasn't something I felt in any specific body part, but I knew that Moira had seen one of the children. I turned to her again, to calculate the direction of her eyes, correcting the angle of mine. On looking again, it was as though the wall of vegetation were beginning to blur, like looking at something when you're very tired, and suddenly, with eerie definition, one object stands out.

Then I saw him.

In the middle of that green nothingness I saw a chin.

A mouth.

A pair of eyes like two sharp pins.

About four years ago, at a wedding banquet for the son of some friends, I was seated at a table with a man wearing a ridiculous bow tie. This was in the last year of Maia's life. My wife's illness had me in a bad mood: all the conversations seemed banal, and 90 percent of the guests insufferably stupid. The girl was no longer a girl and had fallen in love with a physics professor. She'd just gone off to live with him, a fact that had both wounded and relieved me in equal measure, since in the previous months I'd become annoyed by the contrast between her lovestruck jitters and her mother's disease. The idea of losing Maia, of facing the loneliness that would inevitably follow her death, made the world seem like a shambolic and pointless place. I was living in a state that I once heard, quite accurately, described as "the arrogance of the sufferer"—a chronic irritation that, after prolonged suffering, makes many people come to believe that their misfortune grants them a sort of moral superiority. Maia and I had very nearly not gone to the wedding, and when we sat at the table and I saw this man in his bow tie, I was on the verge of telling her we should leave. Two minutes later, it was me who didn't want to leave. He turned out to be charming and funny, and also, for some reason, he treated my wife with extraordinary tenderness. I was touched by this. Illness, or contact with illness, creates strange bedfellows. At the end of the meal, and after a number of jokes about the newlyweds, he got a bit more serious and asked a curious question:

"What would happen if we got a sign the first time we saw the person who was to be the most decisive in our lives?"

"What kind of sign?" Maia asked.

"Not necessarily anything physical. There's no reason it would have to be a light or a sound, but something clear, something *certain,* something that let us know that this person would be part of each one of our decisions, forever."

One person at the table responded, saying that such a

feeling, though perhaps not entirely certain, already existed in the form of intuition, of love at first sight. But the man in the bow tie shook his head.

"I'm not talking about love, of course. I'm talking about a *witness.*"

And then he put forth a theory as twisted as his bow tie: everyone has their own witness. Someone that we secretly want to convince, someone all of our actions are directed toward, someone we can't stop secretly talking to. This witness, he added, is not the most obvious, is almost never your spouse or father or sister or lover, is often someone trivial, secondary to the normal course of life.

I felt as though, of all those seated at the table, only I understood what he was trying to say.

In the yawning silence that followed this monologue I saw the face of Jerónimo Valdés. Jerónimo Valdés had been my witness for the preceding fifteen years of my life (he was still alive then, locked up in the local prison, one of his many stints in jail). It struck me that, just as this man said, I'd felt something like a sign the first time I saw him, during that jungle sweep fifteen years earlier when the dog stared straight into the mass of foliage before me and Jerónimo's features seemed to emerge from the leaves. Jerónimo Valdés was twelve years old at the time, but so short and skinny he could easily have passed for nine. He had an angular, squirrel-like face and eyes the same shade of brown as his hair, as though nature had painted him three colors: the bright white of his teeth, the dark brown of his hair and the caramel of his skin and lips.

He was twenty or so meters from me, totally immobile. His white T-shirt was covered in grime and he was staring straight at me. He looked nimble, like a little fawn, an animal that can jump ten times its own height. There was a sign, but I'm not sure what it was or why we remained silent for so long. I don't know how much time actually passed or if it was simply the adrenaline that expanded my awareness of those seconds. I didn't blow the whistle, despite holding it between my teeth. It was the shock that stopped me, that and the sense that the boy was silently begging me not to. For an instant it seemed that his lightness was somehow dependent on my weight, that I was the gravity keeping him rooted to the earth. I held the dog tightly to keep her from charging, but a second later it was me who began to chase the boy. Jerónimo turned and ran.

My memory of the chase is that it was not long, which I also know by the signs it left on my body; I scratched my face and at some point must have banged my knee, because the next day it was swollen. When Moira got in my way I accidentally kicked her, and she howled plaintively in response. Three steps later I caught Jerónimo for the first time, grabbed him by the T-shirt, and we both nearly tripped; then he broke free and got away. We ran a few meters and finally I managed to grab an arm, but he started kicking, hard. It reminded me of the feeling I'd gotten a few months earlier on catching that girl listening to Maia play the violin in our back garden; more than a child, he seemed like some gigantic insect, a creature with eight or ten limbs flailing desperately in unthinkable directions, each tipped with a small hook, something that stung or scratched. He gave off a sour smell, like the homeless people in town but with a sweeter note, like long-expired yogurt.

When I managed to sit up slightly and looked at his free hand, I saw what had happened: Jerónimo's palm was covered in blood, the knuckles white because he was tightly clenching a small knife, the size of a lollipop. He'd sunk it into my arm twice, and in the excitement I hadn't realized. We both froze expectantly for a second, scandalized, he at having stuck his knife into me, and I at not having noticed anything but the sudden metallic taste in my mouth. After this moment of chaos, he tried again to stab me, this time in the chest, but I grabbed his hand forcefully, jerking his thumb back violently toward his wrist until he let out a yelp and dropped the knife. His face was specked with gravel, like the kind used to cover a patio, his hair stiffer than steel wool. On his upper lip a disconcertingly dark cold sore, or some sort of burn, glistened.

"You're not going to move," I said, unable to hold his stare. "Do you hear me?"

But Jerónimo said nothing.

People are never accepted as innocent the first time around; the greatest punishment is not having to prove yourself but having to do so over and over again. Perhaps that's what I would have liked to have said to the bow-tied sage: that our witnesses are not to blame for the fact that something in us chose them as our unassailable interlocutor, that when it comes down to it, we are the ones who impose this pretense. No one can sustain authenticity forever, not even child witnesses.

Jerónimo had a kind of classic beauty about him. Like all Ñeê children, he had an undeniably photogenic face, in contrast to his actual character, which was austere and headstrong. He rarely smiled, but when he did, his smile was stunning, and although he liked jokes, he made the mistake of always taking them seriously, proving that in this, too, he was a true San Cristóbalite. He was the fourth child of a couple of local tea farmers and had been begging on the city's streets since he learned to walk. His life was like the sounds you hear in a dream, very unusual, which is why I wasn't surprised that he'd joined the thirty-two at the start. He appears in many of the classic images: with the kids running out after the Dakota Supermarket attack, in several undated stills reproduced for Valeria Danas's documentary, and so on. In each of them he looks slightly detached, always at a short distance from the group, but despite this he shows no sign of being ostracized and in fact quite the opposite: he looks distinguished, as though the other children are admiring some quality in him.

Years later, on one of my visits to the local penitentiary (Jerónimo was twenty at the time and back in prison, this time for armed robbery), I asked him what he'd felt when I caught him that day in the jungle. He gave what for him was a detailed response, given that he was inclined to be elusive and monosyllabic when talking about those years, saying that he knew something was going to happen to him and that he'd been afraid the entire night. He couldn't remember why he was alone or what he'd been doing there, so far from the other kids. And I really believe he couldn't remember. Jerónimo Valdés would rather remain silent than have to lie, and whenever he talked about that period, the aggressive way he stared at me on those first few occasions came back. But his aggression never turned to hatred, and I certainly felt nothing like hatred for him.

Perhaps it's impossible to understand and forgive others without having first forgiven and understood oneself. When I grabbed his hand, jamming his thumb back to his wrist hard enough to break it, and blew the whistle between my teeth as loud as possible, I was so aware that I was sentencing him that I couldn't hold his gaze.

Whatever happened the rest of that day has remained in my memory a nebulous smattering of certainties. I know that at some point I lost consciousness and was taken out on a stretcher to the provincial hospital, where I arrived having lost a liter of blood. I know that when I regained consciousness Maia and the girl were by my side and that the girl was watching me with huge, frightened eyes. On seeing me injured, she stopped being almost a teenager for a moment and the girl reemerged. Her eyes filled with tears and she threw her arms around my neck to give me a kiss. Maia told me I'd been sleeping for twelve hours, because on arriving I'd had a breakdown (of which I have no memory) and the doctor had been forced to sedate me. She also told me that they'd finished the sweep and hadn't found any children.

"What about the one I found?"

"Just the one," she amended, "the one you found."

"They really didn't find any?"

Maia did not reply, as was her habit when I asked a redundant question. My zen little wife.

"Does it hurt?" she asked.

It was as if I really had to think about my replies, even to the most basic questions. I tried to recall the face that just a few hours earlier had been only centimeters from mine, but was unable to conjure an accurate picture. All I could remember was that Jerónimo's lightness, his weightlessness, more than a physical characteristic, struck me as a state of being, like the first time you hold a bird in your hand and feel the nervous palpitations of its tiny beating heart. I saw where the knife had entered my right arm for the first time, one wound on the forearm and another larger, semicircular one on my biceps. It was the nagging pain of a broken bone, and Maia told me that according to the doctor I should consider myself a lucky man, that a few centimeters to the right and the knife would have sliced clear through the radial and medial arteries, which would have caused three times the blood loss—in other words, certain death.

Half an hour later Amadeo Roque turned up in my hospital room and told me that the boy I'd found was named Jerónimo Valdés, that he'd been identified by his family from a photo *El Imparcial* had published. It seemed the boy wanted nothing to do with them, and his parents (who had come in only because of all the publicity, and their fear of legal repercussions), on seeing there was no action being taken, didn't want much to do with him either. They swore he'd always been a violent boy and had once tried to kill his younger brother. Since being put in a cell he'd been in a semi-feral state, wasn't eating, had to be forcibly bathed and answered every question he was asked "in an unintelligible language." Amadeo Roque himself looked awful too, as though he hadn't slept in three days, and the heat had given his skin a cerulean hue, as if he were melting from the inside out. The city—he went on telling me—was on the verge of a clash like the one in Plaza Casado, but with added animosity over the search's failure. There had been

a break-in at a home appliance store and two armed rob-
beries at a gas station. The national government was on the
verge of sending reinforcements from police forces in other
cities of the province. The jungle children had disappeared.
Literally. Jerónimo Valdés was refusing to talk. We'd hit a
dead end.

On March 13, 1995, two days after the sweep, I left the hospital with my arm in a sling and headed to the police station where Jerónimo Valdés was locked up. The wound on my arm was still intensely painful, and the mayor had phoned half an hour earlier to tell me he was holding the kid there.

"It doesn't seem very easy to get him to talk."

I asked the mayor to let me be on the interrogation team, led at the time by Amadeo Roque, and he gave me fortyeight hours; after that, the boy would be remanded, which meant he would be in isolation at the juvenile detention center until his Rehabilitation Board interview. By this point it seemed the mayor was largely indifferent to everything.

"I don't think it'll do much good," he said, "but if you want to, have at it."

I once read that a Hindu sage attributed every misfortune that befell him over the course of his life to having stoned a water snake for the fun of it as a boy, killing it. Who can say for sure that Maia's disease, the distance with which my daughter now treats me, or my indifference to the world's beauty don't stem from having kept a boy named Jerónimo Valdés awake for forty hours?

The idea came to me almost inadvertently, after my phone conversation with the mayor, recalling how close I'd once come to the brink of insanity when, after two consecutive nights of insomnia, I had a seemingly endless plane trip. I remembered that toward the end, when I'd gone nearly thirty-five hours straight with no sleep, after having blown up at a flight attendant, I felt my body surrender, felt it break. I don't know exactly how to explain it, but I thought I heard a click, which made me think I was going to have a heart attack, and then something like anguish clutched at my throat. People around me began to stare, their faces dumbfounded, and the drone of the plane engines was so loud that the pain was almost physical. I remember truly believing that if I didn't get to sleep in the next five minutes

I was going to swallow my tongue, a nonsensical fear that made me sob disconsolately. Right then, the flight attendant I'd insulted did something very human, truly touching. She approached with a pillow and an extra blanket, asked me to come with her and led me to a couple of empty seats at the back of the plane. I followed like a zombie. She raised the armrest so I could get comfortable and told me to lie down. It might sound untrue, but I've never been so grateful. I nearly threw myself at her feet weeping; seeing how desperate I was, she stayed with me and even spread the blanket over me. When I saw this, a second before closing my eyes, I thought that I would do anything she asked of me, literally anything.

Walking to the police station, I worked out that Jerónimo Valdés must have been so tired that all I'd have to do was keep him up one night. Beyond that, my plan was not very original: good cop, bad cop. The bad cop would be Amadeo Roque, and he'd wake Jerónimo up again and again; the good cop, who would let him sleep, was me, and I would pretend to be a parent of one of the thirty-two. My idea was to convince him I was Antonio Lara's father. We would both ask the same question over and over, whether letting him sleep or waking him up: *Where are the others?* It was important for there to be no variations, for the question to be identical each time: *Where are the others? Where are the others? Where are the others?* These days repeating it twice is enough for it to pound in my ears like the metallic sound of a trepan. *Where are the others?*

When we got to the cell I was surprised to see how small Jerónimo was. Could this really be the same boy who'd nearly killed me in the jungle? But after studying him at length, he regained that initial elegance. The boy had refused to eat almost anything for two days, and yet, far from looking vulnerable, his appearance was surprisingly dignified. I'd never seen a boy like him. He gave the impression he'd been born there, had always lived and thought right there, had never had a care beyond that of mere survival. His expressions were both touching and primal. I asked that we be left alone and sat down beside him. I asked if he remembered me, showed him my arm and the wound, and reminded him that he'd been the one to do that to me, to which he replied with a look of utter incredulity. He no longer smelled bad, instead gave off a faintly soapy smell, and his hair was carefully brushed, but with the cold sore on his lip, his face still had a sort of spiritual air, like a boy Lazarus brought back from the dead. I pulled the photo of Antonio Lara from my pocket and showed it to him. He took the photo in his hands to look at it up close. His head was bent over, so I couldn't see his expression.

"That's my son," I lied.

He turned suddenly to me, as though Antonio Lara were

some sort of demon. I couldn't have said whether his expression was one of admiration or fear, but there's no doubt that Jerónimo was surprised.

"Don't you want to help me find him?"

He didn't reply, and I lay my uninjured hand on his shoulder. I was moved that he let me leave it there without jerking away or objecting.

It wasn't easy. After ten hours Jerónimo began to fall asleep. The first thing we did was take the cot from his cell and leave only a chair, but the boy took his shirt off, spread it out on the floor like a yogi and tried to go to sleep on top of it. Amadeo Roque let him doze off and then walked into the cell, slamming the door. Jerónimo jumped and dragged himself under the chair. I watched this unfold from behind the tinted glass on the cell door. It was all absurdly schematic: boy, chair, toilet, sink.

Whenever I'm tempted to feel superior to anyone, all I have to do is remember that I tortured a boy, for two days, to get him to give his friends away. It was sort of like the awkward silence that sometimes pervades unhappy families, silence that is far worse than fighting or openly arguing. Every time Jerónimo started falling asleep, Amadeo Roque would come in and shake him, and then I'd walk in and ask: *Where are the others? Aren't you going to help me find my son?* I'd let him lie down on the floor, pretend I would allow him to sleep and even stroke his head as his eyes closed, only for Amadeo Roque to come back twenty minutes later and repeat the entire process.

I remember the dry feel of Jerónimo's hair, I remember distance and proximity, the oil and water of feelings and conscience. Sometimes simply recollecting the scene makes me feel such disgust that my stomach turns, but generally I perceive it with a kind of bewilderment, unable to shake the feeling that the man who did those things was not me but someone else, someone different whose every feeling I somehow recognize and can recall. Jerónimo was a different boy, too, not the teenager he later became or the young child I visited in jail, perhaps not even the actual kid who'd lived with the other boys and girls but instead some force of nature that I attempted to subdue. But whereas the chief of police and I were using the logic of pragmatism and desperation, Jerónimo used that of instinct and loyalty.

Many years after the death of the thirty-two, I read about a biological experiment in which researchers took half a dozen flies and half a dozen bees, put them all in a glass bottle and lay it on its side with the bottom facing a window, to see which ones would escape first. The flies managed to get out by flying away from the window, but the bees died, colliding with one another over and over again at the bottom of the bottle: they could not shake the belief that the exit had to be where the light was shining from. Those bees made me think of the shame I felt back then at the fact that Jerónimo never stopped believing in me. I couldn't understand him, of course. He spoke to me in that language that sounded like twittering, full of absurd sounds. He never stopped believing that I was the one protecting him, a conviction that filtered into his genetic makeup the way vice takes root in a strong-willed person. I was the light that his brain kept colliding with. Every time he saw me arrive, his face softened. If I'd walked into the cell and told him the sun had gone out, he would have believed me. I now understand (it turns out that understanding, more than a talent, is a discipline) that his belief was as monstrous as the torture we subjected him to over those nearly two days. Perhaps that belief was nature's way of punishing me. Regardless of the name my imagination gives it, regardless of how many years have passed, it's still just as painful to me.

And then finally he gave in.

It was only a matter of time, we knew this, and yet when it actually happened we were as amazed as if we'd seen a miracle. It was forty hours after our torture had begun, almost nightfall on the second day. I walked into the cell and knew immediately that something had changed. Jerónimo's lip was quivering like jelly, and he started tracing one eyebrow with his fingertip, a gesture that struck me as both delicate and adult. He said a couple of things in that incomprehensible language and I responded the same as always, telling him that I didn't understand what he was saying. He traced his eyebrow once more. The police doctor had told us that after a time the boy might begin hallucinating, and this would be an indisputable sign that his health was at risk. For a moment I was afraid he might do something rash. I went to him and placed a hand on his shoulder, but he shook it off instantly. Over the previous few hours he'd been scratching himself, and his leg jiggled anxiously like a boy taking an exam.

I asked if he was hungry and, though he made no reply, asked that he be brought a sandwich and a glass of water. For the first time he ate with real gusto, but every time he took a drink his expression became absent, like a person searching for words they've forgotten. There was a split second when I thought he was blushing. When Jerónimo finished eating he calmly stood, put his plate on the floor and pulled the chair over to the cell window, which looked out onto the street. He wouldn't let me help him climb onto it, but managed by himself, grabbing the window bars with both hands. Jerónimo beckoned me over. Then he spoke in that incomprehensible language again. It was almost a whisper.

"I can't understand you, Jerónimo," I said yet again, whispering as well.

Jerónimo turned to me. I felt afraid. The bags under his eyes were almost violet, and slightly glossy. He seemed surprised to see me, to see himself, to be up on that chair looking out through the window bars.

"Where are the others?" I repeated.

And he turned back to the window, pointed to the sewer and for the first time speaking perfect Spanish, he whispered:

"There. They're in there."

Like someone discovering a betrayal, I was overwhelmed by the feeling that there had to have been signs, that the past must have been rife with signs: the noise on the patio that I'd attributed to rats, the overturned trash bins outside the supermarket ... There are certain things that people understand only when they're ready to accept them, but at times I wonder if it wasn't that our minds chose to ignore the clearest signs that the children were living in the sewers. I tell myself that there were (there *must* have been) people in the city who saw them and said nothing. Often we submit to the prevailing morality only because the truth seems less plausible than the beliefs we adopt. After all, can we really put so much faith in things we see — as is often said so dramatically — *with our own eyes*?

We avoided the temptation to charge headlong into the sewers because by that point the possibility of landing in jail if any of the children were hurt was too real. And there was also a real fear, a fear that pervaded everything and bordered on a dreamlike state. It was so pure it seemed to buzz in our ears. We convened a crisis cabinet and spread the sewer map out on Amadeo Roque's desk. It was a star-shaped system and flowed east beneath the city: six canals converging in an enormous drainpipe over the river Eré. We didn't know exactly where the children were, but deduced by the dimensions and height of the tunnels (in many places under half a meter) that there were only four spots where they could be, all of them close and all interconnected, coinciding with the riverwalk and the area surrounding Plaza 16 de Diciembre.

More than feeling uneasy, it was as though we were drugged. Ideas were notably lacking. Amadeo Roque suggested entering directly through city hall's sewers, and one imbecile proposed smoking the kids out, asphyxiating them by starting a fire. It was Alberto Ávila — one of the district police chiefs — who suggested closing off every way out of Zone T (the quadrant where we presumed they were) and then entering the sewers at equidistant points a hundred meters apart, to comb the tunnels until we converged in a single enclosed area.

Many years later I learned from Jerónimo Valdés that we'd got it right only by chance. During the first weeks the children lived in the sewers they weren't in that quadrant but the northeastern one, which of course made sense: it was the one closest to the jungle. According to Jerónimo, they'd moved after one of the girls had died from a snakebite. He confessed that before moving to the sewers under the city they buried her by the derelict picnic area, using random bricks they found lying around. A week after the entire ordeal ended I went there with the head of Social Affairs and two medical examiners to recover and identify the body; it was just us. For six days, the media had done nothing but show the infamous photo of thirty-two corpses lined up along the riverwalk, which meant that nobody cared too much about one extra body, so out of place. We found it exactly where Jerónimo had said we would. And indeed it was a girl; she couldn't have been more than ten years old. They'd entombed her in the fetal position to minimize the size of the structure required. She was covered with a blanket and surrounded by what looked to be scraps of food and small toys. Over the months she'd been there, given the jungle's humidity, her body had decomposed unevenly and was partially covered in brown spots while other parts remained intact. In her left hand she held three Playmobil dolls, and when the pathologist took them from her to examine them, I got the unsettling sense that he'd committed a desecration. There was a large Z on her forehead, and death had given her an almost petulant expression. Her left ankle was shockingly black, and the swelling from the snakebite that had killed her was visible. Around the bite were drawings done with markers—a rainbow of sorts, and stars that ran up her leg to her stomach, where someone had drawn a large sun and written her name: Ana. The reality of this girl's death, her body disinterred only a week after her companions had died, seemed to lead to a place we'd never have dared to explore even had we been able. This wasn't simply the burial of one child carried out by other children, but something as incomprehensible and yet as tangible as proof of another civilization. Another world.

We finally opted for Alberto Ávila's plan.

By ten in the morning on March 19, 1995, we'd clamped shut every channel out of San Cristóbal's sewer system and stationed police at each manhole of the area where we assumed the children were. The belief was that realizing they were surrounded would naturally lead them to gather in the same underground location, where all channels met in a sort of vault that the map showed as being pentagonal.

The operation began at eleven thirty on one of the hottest days I can recall having endured in San Cristóbal. The heat index was 100 degrees, with 87 percent humidity. It was a Thursday and the city was bustling, in full commercial swing. We descended into the sewers pretending to be city workers, without attracting anyone's attention. As is often the case, something that would have aroused suspicion at night, when done in broad daylight, and in full view of everyone, did not. We split into seven groups. My party was to cover a kilometer and a half of the eastern canal and was comprised of four police officers, one Social Services health worker and me. Some of the groups included the children's family members: Antonio Lara was one of them, and Pablo Flores was in charge of group 4, the one traversing the entire first channel up to the intersection where we assumed we would find the children, and where, if the plan worked, they would end up cornered. Above this spot, three patrol cars and two Department of Social Affairs vans waited.

As I climbed down the ladder, grabbing hold of the metal bars, searing pain shot through the wound on my arm and I thought of Jerónimo Valdés with hatred. This was the first time I'd been in a sewer, and though the smell was not pleasant, it was far less intense than I'd imagined: the canals were dry and better ventilated than I had assumed, and the few rats we saw elicited more jubilation than disgust. We humans are strange creatures, enthusiastic at the sight of what we already know we'll see.

We carried flashlights and wore headlamps, but much of

the time there was no need to turn them on: light filtered in from the manholes above, creating an eerie effect throughout the corridor, as though it were being lit by angled stage lights. The corridors branching off to the sides (which according to the map joined our canal to the others via a large spiderweb pattern) bore metal plates with the names of the corresponding streets aboveground. Under one of these plates we got our first sign of the children: an enormous chalk drawing of a bird, its wings spread. Multiple veins emerged from the bird's heart and traveled up its wings.

This may sound farfetched, but it was looking at that bird that made me wonder for the first time if the children hated us. If they hated us in the way that perhaps only children can hate. We know what children's love is like, but our ideas about their hatred are rudimentary and often incorrect: we think that in children the feeling is mixed with fear, and therefore with fascination, and thus perhaps with love, or some type of love, as well; that children's hatred is made up of channels that connect different sentiments to one another and something causes them to move toward it.

I asked Jerónimo about this emotion for years, and in many different ways, always avoiding the word "hate." Not once did he respond directly. It wasn't simply his reticence about all things sentimental—the experience ended up providing me with ways to get him to talk about many other things, even when he didn't want to—but something much darker that I learned to respect: succor. I realized that children's privacy is like a cry for help. Someone stops before danger and asks for help. One is strong and the other weaker, but unlike with adults, in children the one who doesn't move is the brave one, the real threat.

And that's where it all began.

In that sentiment, that *exact place*.

The only consequential part of the Valeria Danas documentary is the interviews with all twenty-six people who'd been inside that "secret city"—as some insisted on calling it —of which there are no remaining images aside from those in our memory. Would we have paid closer attention had we known we'd get to see it for only a few minutes? I have absolutely no doubt.

My group wasn't the first to arrive; when we arrived at least ten people were already there, awestruck. The room was a ninety-square-meter pentagon, three meters high, illuminated by the daylight filtering in from four manholes above. The first impression was marvelous. There were hundreds of small pieces of mirror and glass everywhere, affixed to the walls with no apparent logic. Bottle necks, cracked eyeglasses, broken lightbulbs caused the light to bounce off some walls onto others as if it were a huge party, with sparkling green, brown, blue and orange, but also some encoded meaning. Many of the pieces rested on what looked almost like built-in shelving, others had been affixed to the sewer walls, and a large blue pane of glass had some-how been attached to one of the manholes and projected blue light all along the ground. The light streaming in must have made objects glimmer in a different way at noon than they did at three. The luminous phrase must have changed over the course of the day, and it gave the impression that the entire patchwork of colored glass, shards of mirror, pieces of magnifying glass and small bottles had been de-signed to create specific shapes: one reflection looked like a face, while others clearly resembled a tree, a dog, a house . . .

Why, when we've so admired cave paintings dating back to the dawn of human consciousness, would we not also admire the extraordinary luminous decor created by the thirty-two in the San Cristóbal sewers for the same reason? While our ancestors drew eight-legged horses in order to simulate movement and used caves' recesses to make bison, the thirty-two had decorated their walls with something far more intangible: light. The stillness of those glimmer-ing objects enveloped us so totally that for a few minutes we hovered in silence. I remember how much I wanted to be alone in that place, which at the time struck me as sacred. In one of the interviews, a woman says something I'll never forget: when the initial shock passed, she says, she was filled with the sense that all of that light had been constructed "with diligence and pleasure." That's it precisely. This lu-minous structure contained pleasure the way an egg contains its yolk. It would have been as impossible to claim the children had done this by accident as it would be to throw a pile of words into the air and expect them to land forming the opening of a story. And in that leap was joy, a radiant and touching childlike joy.

Jerónimo would never talk about the glass. Only once did he confess that he personally had stuck some of the pieces to the wall and that at certain times of day, though not every day, the children played a game, but he refused to explain what the game was. A passing comment led me to believe that this cathedral of light had been designed in completely democratic fashion. There was no mastermind in the shadows, only a sort of collective and impartial love of play — "pleasure," as the woman in the documentary says. The remaining witnesses' comments are contradictory and at times slightly affected. Some people claim that the glass "tinkled." I recall no such thing. What's more, most of it wasn't hanging from the walls but *embedded into* them, which supports Valeria Danas's hypothesis that the sewer topography rather than the children's creativity determined the shape of this work of luminous art, although we know how keen Valeria Danas can be to deny us even the most basic of magic. The first time I heard this opinion I disagreed, and now I disagree still more. Over the years, my memory of some things has grown hazy, but I feel that today I see more clearly a shape, something like a rectangle that led to a door, a simple shape not very different from the one Rothko painted over and over and which looked as though it had been made deliberately. Perhaps it was a mere accident of the topography, but I have a hard time believing that. The pentagonal chamber, covered in mirrors and glass and pieces of tin and broken eyeglasses, was the closest thing imaginable to a body. And it was inside this body, as if within its heart, that the thirty-two lived. The idea is so simple I've often felt as if it were burning me.

Neither the layout nor the height of the place seemed to respond to any pragmatic need. True, many of the city's gas pipelines and one of the biggest generators in the northern sector converged there, but this didn't explain the pentagonal shape and certainly not the many shelf-like niches in the wall. For years people speculated over whether the place had been a storeroom built to warehouse supplies during the sewer's construction, which would at least have explained the niches. Many of us were so bedazzled by the reflecting light that we didn't notice, didn't spot the niches. There were (or *are,* since they're still there) more than thirty of them, each over a meter and a half long and one meter deep. The kids apparently slept on them in relatively random fashion.

What a strange and careful republic all of those little beds made. The Valeria Danas documentary has a shot of the place, but one taken long after the altercations, and needless to say, it shows no sign of the lives of the thirty-two. A deceitful image, like every image of an empty home. The witnesses' comments are more real: some describe it as an "asymmetrical colony," others — more rightly — say it looked like a family pantheon. And while it did indeed resemble a columbarium, it also could have been bunk beds, or one of those boxes typesetters store text characters in. Even the sense that one child slept in each niche was misleading: clothes were all tangled together and sometimes seemed to belong to various children. Some of the niches were so hard to reach that I can't imagine how they managed to climb up to them without breaking their necks, and there were little things, small treasures, scattered on all of them: bottle caps, pebbles, candy, a brooch, belt buckles . . . I remember very few of the things I saw; in my mind they're all one big jumble. The only thing I'm sure of is that the objects were *there,* treasures slowly amassed, imbued with the children's desires. Jerónimo once told me that they had stopped using money (our money) early on, but they never stopped bartering, small objects and favors. Maybe those seemingly random objects were actually their currency. The children had fled their city so quickly that they'd left their money behind.

What were their lives like? The same way you sometimes walk into a person's house and get a feeling, an accurate picture of the activities of those who live there, the rules and laws they live by, this place, too, seemed to contain the spirit of their movements. You could sense it in the simple way that being in one place (by the panel full of pipes, for instance) invited you to walk someplace else (under the blue light projected from the ceiling). For years, every time I thought of the huge space where the thirty-two lived, what instantly came to mind was a house where I spent part of my child-hood, an old country house with a circular layout where — inexplicably — in order to get to the dining room you had to walk through one of the bedrooms. My mother always com-plained about how nonsensical the floor plan was, but for some reason she never did anything to change it. Now it oc-curs to me that she didn't change it because that layout was the one most befitting the actual house, and therefore we ended up adapting ourselves to it. Some houses make their inhabitants live like reptiles, others like men, others like in-sects. Regardless of how unlikely it was that the architects who'd designed the sewer system had imagined that a com-munity of thirty-two children would end up living in it, this place, too, was predetermined, and the children ended up adapting to the spirit it imposed on them. All you had to do was slowly close your eyes to get used to the darkness and see that the space worked as an enormous bedroom. Those of us there had come in by walking through openings in the corridors, and we'd instantly realized, without anyone ex-plaining: the room was a giant, warm bedroom. A dilation. The body opened up to embrace its guests, and embracing its guests filled them with the illusory sense that the cement walls were in fact soft and yielding.

Jerónimo spoke to me once about the sounds there. He'd just turned seventeen and was being transferred from the juvenile detention center to a trade school where, in theory, he would study carpentry. He'd refused his family's visits and asked that I be named his legal guardian. I wasn't expecting this and was so touched by the gesture that I was glad not to have been notified of it in his presence, since my eyes welled up. Jerónimo had turned into a relatively attractive young man, but he was so quiet that his silence inevitably generated hostility in those around him. He was sometimes violent, and I suspect that his life in the reformatory wasn't exactly easy, but he never complained about anything. Being the only survivor, his karma weighed on him so heavily at first that he'd gotten used to being alone; four years after the death of the thirty-two, he was still cagey. I remember bringing him a gift that day, a penknife I'd found at a flea market, a sort of coarse antique in the shape of a girl. I knew that kids in the reformatory weren't allowed to receive this kind of thing, but Jerónimo was not a normal kid, and nor, most definitely, was my relationship with him. He was fascinated by it and stared at the crude shape as though hypnotized by a miniature brass siren. I remember we sat on one of the benches at the detention center and he started jabbing the knife into the wood. This was the first time he talked about the sounds inside the sewer. It wasn't me who asked (despite having done so and receiving no reply hundreds of times before), and he told me that some nights, as he and the other kids slept in the niches, he thought he heard a hoarse voice speaking to him, the voice of a monster. I don't recall Jerónimo's exact words, but I do recall his distress at listening to that voice: he said it was like a face with no precise shape, except for a very clear mouth and a long, thin mustache. A real mouth. He also said that other kids heard the voice too, and that everyone was afraid of it. "It would wake you up in the middle of a dream and tell you things." I asked him what things, but he didn't answer. I asked him what they did when they were afraid, and he said, Be together and tell stories. That was all.

Learning about that fear totally sabotaged my memory of that day. In the same way people think back about someone they saw or interacted with, someone about to get divorced or to die without knowing it, and in retrospect they think the person's face showed clear signs, I remembered what my transformation was like, the one that occurred when I saw the word "whore" written in chalk next to one of those niches. I remembered this while speaking to Jerónimo, four years later. I remembered that some of the beds still bore the shape of a child's head and others seemed to have been rummaged through, in search of something. I remembered that the air had an intensely sour smell, like rotting food, like cigarettes, and that to avoid seeing the word again I looked back up at the light and tried to reconstruct the contours of a girl, a boy, lost in the light of those reflections, children awestruck at the beauty and the chaos and the darkness and the wonder. But the word was too persistent. For a second I seemed to perceive everything: I thought I saw them, their presence like a glow, and I saw the roaring freedom of this place that seemed to have been built just for them before the world was created. I saw how things had begun as a game, maybe in one of those corners where there were still a few toys, no doubt stolen from some patio, or perhaps brought from their own homes. This artificial world, filled with miracles, revelations and camaraderie. I put my hand on one of the niches and knew that two children had slept there, arms around each other. I could still see their curved outlines and the way one's head was tilted, resting on the back or shoulder of the other. Two children had shared this niche and had fallen asleep with their eyes open, staring up at the glass as it cast reflections in the shape of a dog, a tree, a house.

But if someone had written the word "whore," then there had also been love: the enormity of one required the viciousness of the other, I thought, trying to breathe. I felt the need to cling to this idea as though to a raft. And if love had existed (it didn't matter in what form), then something had remained intact. Physical love, the love of camaraderie,

sexual love in all of its awkward and no doubt tentative primal expressions, had to have existed there; wasn't the word
"whore" undeniable proof of that? Now I didn't know
what to think. I was like someone who's dropped something of great value—a ring, a diamond—on the beach,
in a dune, and begins combing through it, parting the sand
here and there with their fingers, so desperate to find it that
they think the tiniest glimmer must be the ring, but no. As
time passes and the object doesn't appear, they reproach
themselves for the search itself, because the search caused it
to become lost; had their fingers not combed so insistently
through the sand, it wouldn't have gotten buried, wouldn't
now be irretrievable. The determined, melancholic existence of the word soiled the expression of love, making it
self-absorbed and empty. The word "whore" made everything disappear, which is why I kept doggedly mining it.
There had been a time—I knew this, knew it with a certainty that shocked me—when the children were there but
that word was not yet written on the wall. The days must
have been slow, but also contained, as they gazed up, cars
driving back and forth (because cars drove over the manholes, making shadows spin throughout the chamber and
giving it the quality of a blink), but the word "whore" made
everything vanish—WHORE, in Spanish, in a child's
trembling hand, the W smaller than the H, the E sort of
closed, its foot curving up and in.

People will think I'm fabricating. Above the word "whore" was what looked like a cot. And on it a shadow, the shadow of a presence slightly larger than the others, almost the length of a teenage girl. And white tennis shoes, or shoes that had once been white, and a thick green T-shirt with butterflies. (The whore's T-shirt, I thought; the whore's tennis shoes.) The word "whore" was the place where the children had gone wrong, gotten lost, the place their community had broken down. What had they thought, those children? That they couldn't go wrong simply by virtue of being children? And there we were, the adults, walking through, engrossed, unspeaking, gazing up and down, crouching over piles of clothing and remnants of canned food, feeling the anguish that was now totally unavoidable, because they'd failed and there was nothing to be done about it.

Someone began to cry, weeping in that graceless way adults do when they feel all hope is lost. No one bothered to console them; we were all too engrossed. That was when I turned and found myself face-to-face with Antonio Lara. In his hand he was clutching a blue T-shirt so tightly that I knew it must have been his son's.

"They're not here," he said.

But he wasn't talking to me. He denied to avoid believing, in the hope that reality would come and say, That's not true. He wasn't the only parent. Pablo Flores was there too, and Matilda Serra and Luis Azaola, parents of the children who had disappeared during the Plaza Casado episode. They were easy to spot, because on reaching the pentagon they'd sought one another out and walked as a compact group, rummaging through the clothes and objects left behind on the niches.

"They're not here," he repeated. Then, still looking at me, he shouted: "Antonio!!"

He shouted "Antonio" as loud as he could, and there came a hollow silence that made our blood run cold. Then he crouched down and, leaning over a tiny hole, a hole barely large enough to fit a cat, he shouted again: "Antonio!!" Pablo Flores, who was next to him, shouted "Pablo!" and then a woman shouted "Teresa!" And at that point the three names being shouted blended together: Antonio, Pablo, Teresa, maybe some other names as well. I began shouting myself. I don't think any of us truly believed this would make them appear, but our shouting produced a familiar, liberating effect—this was our language, our logic. Our cries were like cries of horror. Was it then that I understood, or was it later? There came an eerie pause. Perhaps only a few minutes went by. We got up and kept searching, walking back toward the corridors we'd emerged from and then turning back around. The shouting began again. Then the silence. A weary silence, detached, like what astronauts must feel in space, a silence unrelated to human life. All that could be heard was the electric clicking of some sort of meter and the oceanlike sound of the cars driving over our heads. I looked for Antonio Lara and found him sitting, covering his face with that T-shirt.

I was surprised when I looked at my watch; we'd been confined there nearly an hour and a half. When it seemed as though we would spend the rest of our lives underground, Amadeo Roque abruptly rose, leaned against one of the niches and shouted that we had to get out of there, that they'd radioed in to say there was a malfunction, something about pressure in the pipes, and it could be dangerous. Nobody was unwilling. In some interviews people say that a few of the parents had to be dragged out, but that is far from the truth. In fact, I'd dare say they were the first to leave. They did so with a slow and uncertain sadness, and I remember that when the four overhead manholes were opened, the bright light was so intense that each of us covered ourselves, as if an evil spirit had stolen our ability to tolerate the sun.

I was one of the last to leave. Nearly everybody was out by the time we heard the cracking sound. And after that crack came an anxious voice, and then a whistle, and after the whistle an unmistakable explosion, an explosion that made the floor tremble like a drum skin.

The Eré River's water is not always brown. On particularly sunny days (and I imagine it also depends on other factors I couldn't identify) it can be a beautiful emerald color. Many people choose to believe that the day the San Cristóbal children drowned, this was the color of the water, but I know full well that when we emerged from the underground sewer, hearts pounding out of our chests, convinced we were about to be electrocuted, what came rushing behind us was an enormous, dense brown regurgitation. The Eré's water is like moving earth, and a beautiful Ñeê legend says that one day, tired of forever seeing the same landscape, the earth went for a walk and thus was born the river.

Many people claim to have heard the children screaming. I was there and cannot say the same. I know what everyone knows at this point: that they became trapped in the lower corridor, where they'd hidden to escape from us, and that it was them—their weight, specifically—that caused the sluice gate to crack, which triggered the flood. They'd slithered through a canal hardly more than a foot and a half tall and into an old repository where they could see us in their chamber. They'd seen us. It's difficult to rid oneself of that notion, that the children were watching us the entire time without saying a word. It's like feeling the pressure of someone's hand on you long after they've removed it. Had we kept quiet for a few more seconds, perhaps we'd have heard them whispering, but we were too noisy in our exclamations of surprise, our cries of anguish. I know some of the parents—Pablo Flores among them—have claimed that at a certain point they "felt" the children's eyes. I cannot say the same. I didn't feel them at the time; it's now that I do, although more than a judgment or a respite, I feel them as a secret. At first it frightened me, but later it changed and became more of a protective gaze, hazy and sentimental. At times I'm even overcome by the impossible feeling that I can see myself there, in that place, awed by the reflections of so many shards of colored glass, as if for a second I could see myself through their eyes.

But the image of all of those children drowning in that brown water is still hard to bear. After a weeklong investigation, experts concluded that the flood had been so quick that the children had no time to return to the upper level. They'd tried to go back the way they came, but the opening was so narrow and the water pressure so intense that they didn't even get close. The forensics report states that it took eight to ten minutes for them to die by drowning. River water flooded their lungs first, and then, by osmosis, entered their bloodstreams. In my ignorance I had always believed that this was the point at which any death by drowning occurred; I didn't realize that what causes death is that once water enters the blood, it dilutes it, and this is in fact what causes the cells to burst. This image of bursting cells troubled me for some time, but in the end this too receded, like so many other things that have troubled me in life: the image of Maia, rigid and afraid, taking her last breath; the day I happened upon Antonio Lara with the girl, sitting in a café chatting; the first time after my wife's death that a woman said she loved me.

Even where the most private of secrets are confided, there is always room to resist, something that goes unconfessed, some tiny sign or gesture that embodies whatever is withheld. I try now to think about what the city of San

Cristóbal withheld from the thirty-two, despite the statue (which was inevitably hideous) erected in their honor in Plaza 16 de Diciembre; despite the newspaper tributes duly lavished on them every March 19 for the first five years and thereafter only every other; and despite the dozens of articles, documentaries and works of art infused with equal parts guilt, bad taste and a good dose of truth.

It doesn't surprise me that Jerónimo Valdés would refuse to discuss the matter, or that after two or three stints in prison he decided, one fine day, to vanish forever and ended up who knows where. I've often thought that when I first came across him in the jungle he also was running away from the other children, and that running and violence were in his nature, just as it is in the nature of the river Eré to sweep away everything in its path. There is, however, one thing that remains, a kind of music. Sometimes it comes to me in the middle of the street, if I'm returning home very late, or when I go out for a stroll; I hear it as if it were coming up through the ground, through my feet, as though the whispered conversations and secrets of the thirty-two were still humming underfoot. But then even that recedes. It may be true that the dead betray us when they abandon us, but we too betray them in order to live.

Keep in touch with
Granta Books:

Visit granta.com to discover more.

GRANTA

Also available from Granta Books
www.granta.com

SUCH SMALL HANDS

Andrés Barba

Translated by Lisa Dillman

Afterword by Edmund White

Marina's father died instantly, her mother in the hospital. Now she lives in the orphanage with the other little girls. But Marina is not like the other little girls.

'Chilling . . . sinister . . . as effective a ghost story as any I have read' Sarah Perry, *Guardian*

'*Such Small Hands* is more than just a scary story . . . This is so much worse' Susan Hill

'Magnificently chilling . . . worthy of the most spine-tingling horror film' *Financial Times*

'Eerie, uncanny . . . [It will] creep deep beneath the skin' *Daily Mail*

'A dark, deft trip to a zone where desire and frenzy meet' Rob Doyle

'Brilliant . . . I'd highly recommend it' Sinéad Gleeson

'Full of magic, malice and troubling enchantment' Colin Barrett

'Chilling' *Mail on Sunday*

'Terrifying but irresistible' *New Statesman*